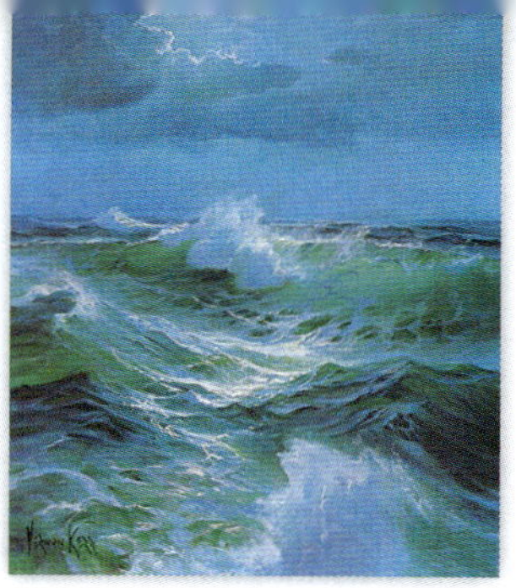

Land and Sea

Nature provides an endless variety of appealing subjects to inspire the artist. And with the versatile medium of oil, you can both layer transparent glazes and apply thick, luscious strokes of color for a wide range of interesting effects. In this book, the artist shows you his step-by-step process for painting seascapes and landscapes in oil, from simple sketches to the most elaborate renderings. In addition, he demonstrates how to capture the beauty of nature in all its seasons and at different times of the day, as well as the importance of making small color studies and learning the various cloud formations. You'll also discover tips for using color effectively, with additional helpful information on composition, perspective, texture, and contrast. And along the way, you'll learn special techniques for creating dramatic skies, luminous waves, and lush landscapes.

CONTENTS

Walter Foster

Starting Procedures:

SURFACES:

I prefer linen canvas or fiberboard panels for quality work, although cotton and other surfaces may be used for practice. Prepare the surfaces as follows:

Smooth Board: Coat the board twice with acrylic gesso, using paint roller or brush. Wipe away the air bubbles. Dry each time and sand lightly.

Textured Canvas: Brush Flake White onto a primed canvas in an irregular pattern and press with a painting knife for a variety of textures.

Textured Board: Coat the board first with acrylic gesso to seal it, then use acrylic modeling paste with a knife and #6 brush to create a combination of textures. EXPERIMENT!

MATERIALS:

Medium: In a squeeze bottle, mix 2 parts turp, 2 parts linseed oil, and 1 part damar varnish. The varnish helps the strokes stay in place. You can adjust amounts for personal preference and drying characteristics.

Brushes: I use lots of brushes to keep the painting fresh, so I don't have to stop to clean during a session. Get as many as you can of flats, brights, filberts, and rounds in sizes 2, 4, 6, 8, 10, 12. Short bristle brushes are for laying on the paint. Long filberts are for blending, because they flex. Rounds (which the Old Masters used) are for rolling on paint and texturing. A one-inch pure-bristle housepainter's sash brush is excellent for blocking in and blending large areas. Small and large fan blenders are for special effects. I also use script liners for twigs and finework, and sables, especially flat sables in sizes from ¼″ to 1″ wide.

Paint: A medium-grade oil paint will save you money and give you good service. Don't scrimp on how much paint you squeeze onto the palette! Use enough to see you through the job. I would rather waste paint than fiddle with a tube in the middle of my creation.

Misc. Materials: Two 16x20 palettes; tissues to keep the brushes clean as you work; charcoal and rags; one small and one large palette knife for painting and mixing paint. You can clean your brushes in fuel oil or kerosene, and dry them with a tissue.

TURPENTINE WASHES:

First sketch lightly with soft charcoal, then wash in major areas with a combination of pure color and turpentine. The turp wash will establish a nice tone to work on and will also remove the glare of a white canvas. Do not use white paint or premixes in the beginning stages of painting.

PREMIXED OILS:

Premixes will make your painting go faster, and will get you better values and colors. Choose a blue, for instance, and blend it with 4 inches of white until it becomes a #2 value (see Value Chart). Set aside half the premix, and mix more blue into the remaining glob until it reaches #5 value. Repeat the procedure for the other main colors on your palette. Now you can use these premixes instead of white, and your colors will be bright, NOT CHALKY. As a last resort, you may use white to lighten a value if needed, but be careful! I recommend leaving it off your palette.

PALETTE SPECTRUM:

THIS IS THE MOST IMPORTANT THING I CAN TEACH YOU IN THIS BOOK! I begin every painting by mixing a color spectrum on a large palette. I squeeze out lots of paint and premixes, and blend their edges together until it represents all of the colors and values which will be in the final painting. When I am on location, I actually hold the palette up in front of me, and if it matches the scene before me, I am ready to begin painting. The value of the spectrum is that it saves time trying to find the right blend of colors, and my painting does not get muddy.

NOW THAT YOU KNOW MY SECRETS,
HAPPY PAINTING!

VERNON KERR

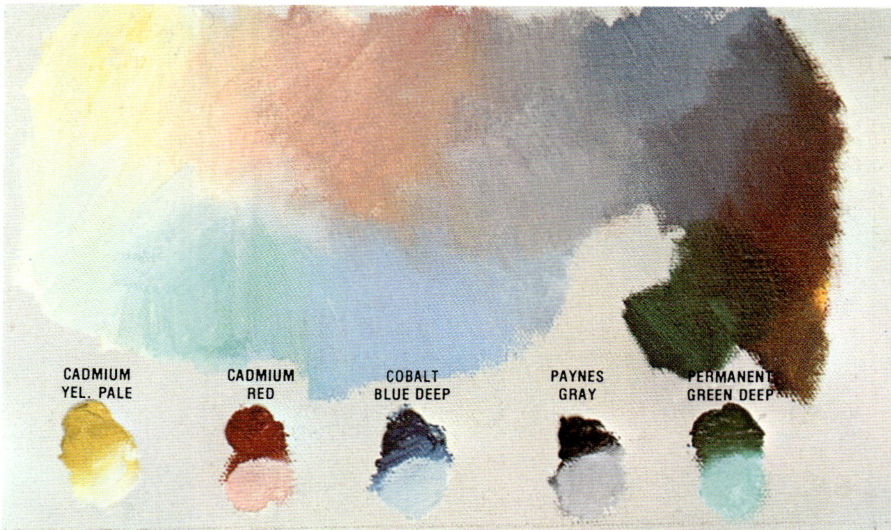

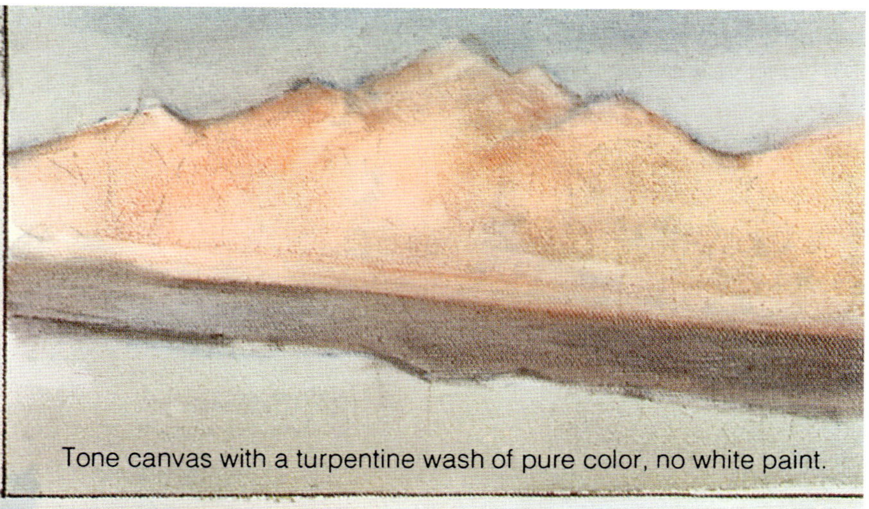

Tone canvas with a turpentine wash of pure color, no white paint.

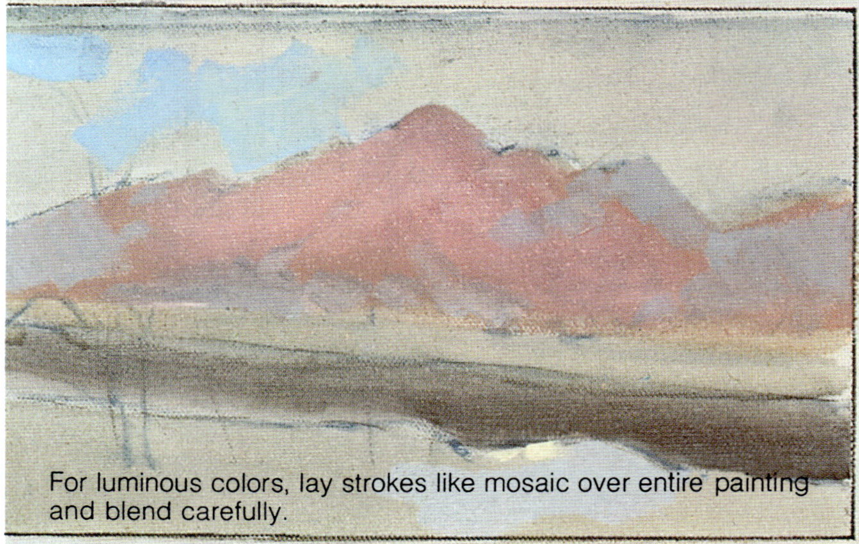

For luminous colors, lay strokes like mosaic over entire painting and blend carefully.

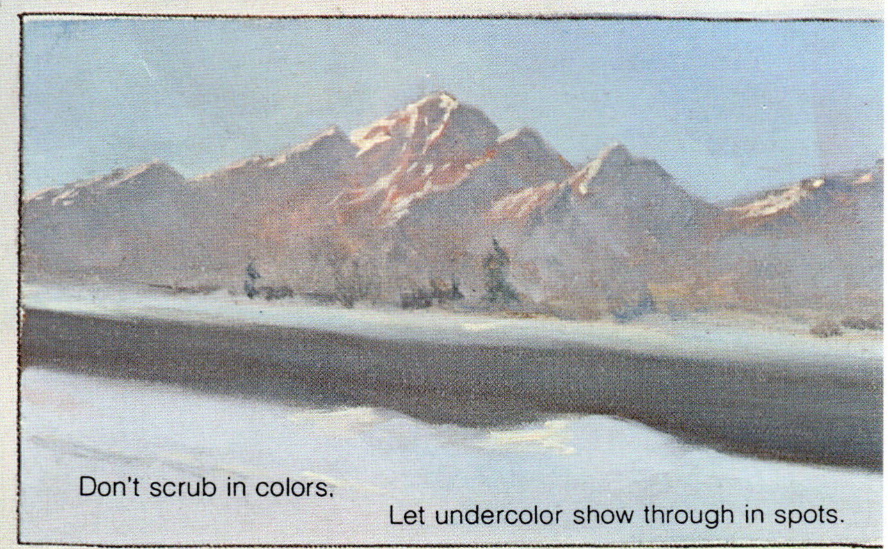

Don't scrub in colors. Let undercolor show through in spots.

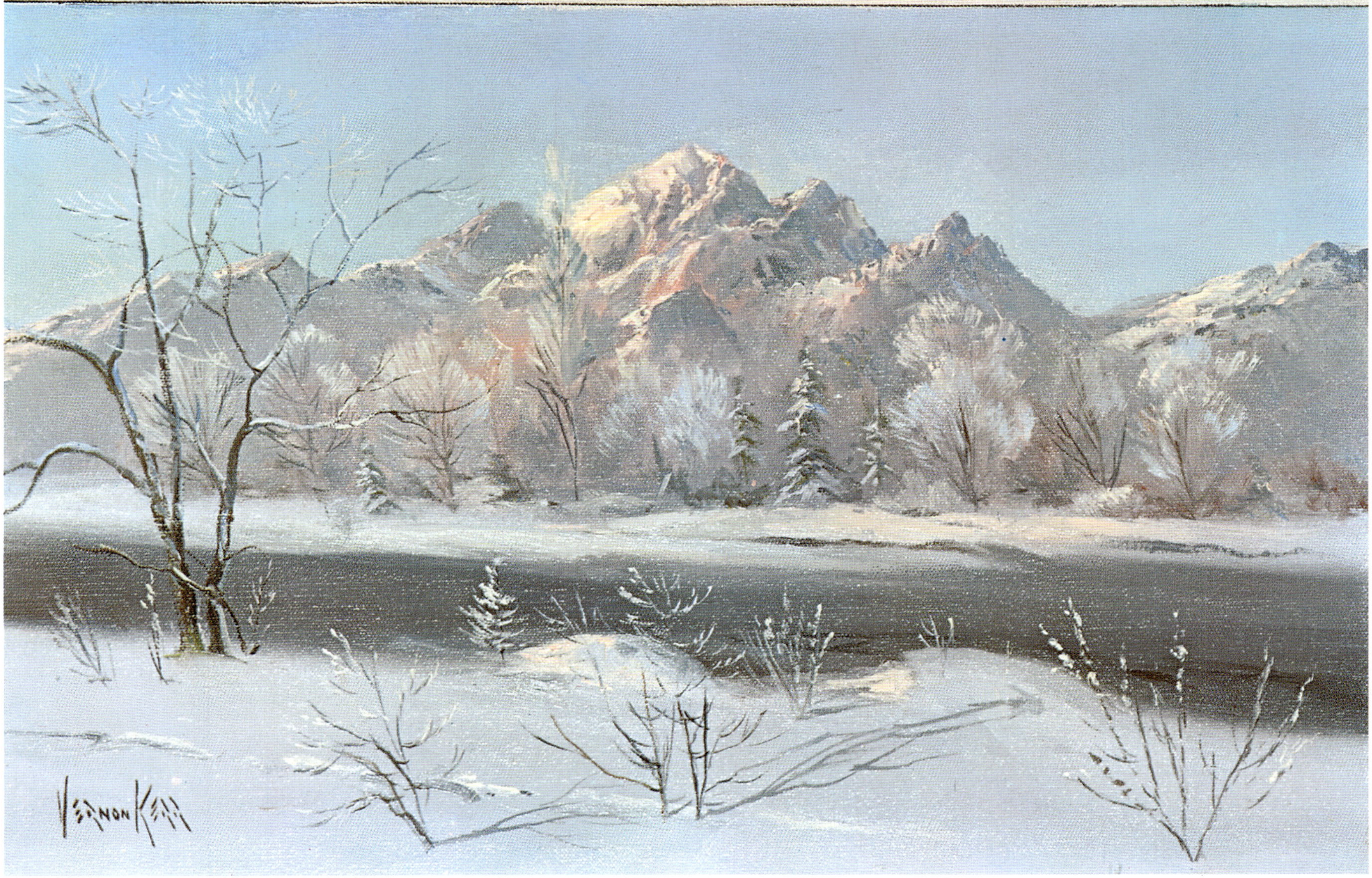

FANTASY MOUNTAIN. Here you can see the value of using premixes in the final stages. Observe the optical illusion achieved by placing a warm tone next to a cool tone of the same value. The mountain is painted wet into wet for subtle blending, but the bushes may be finished after the mountain is dry. To paint into a dry picture, apply a mixture of half turp and half linseed oil over the entire canvas, and then wipe it off. Thin limbs in the sky area look more convincing if they are soft blue-gray, not brown.

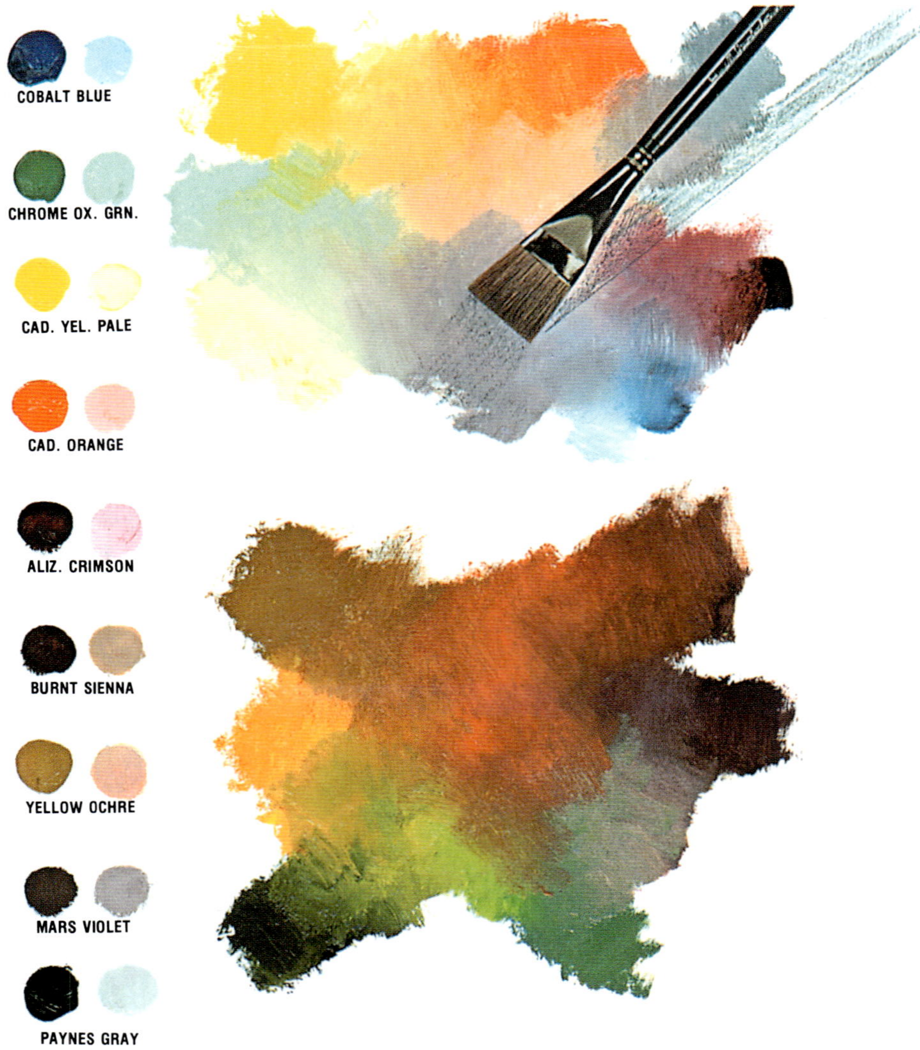

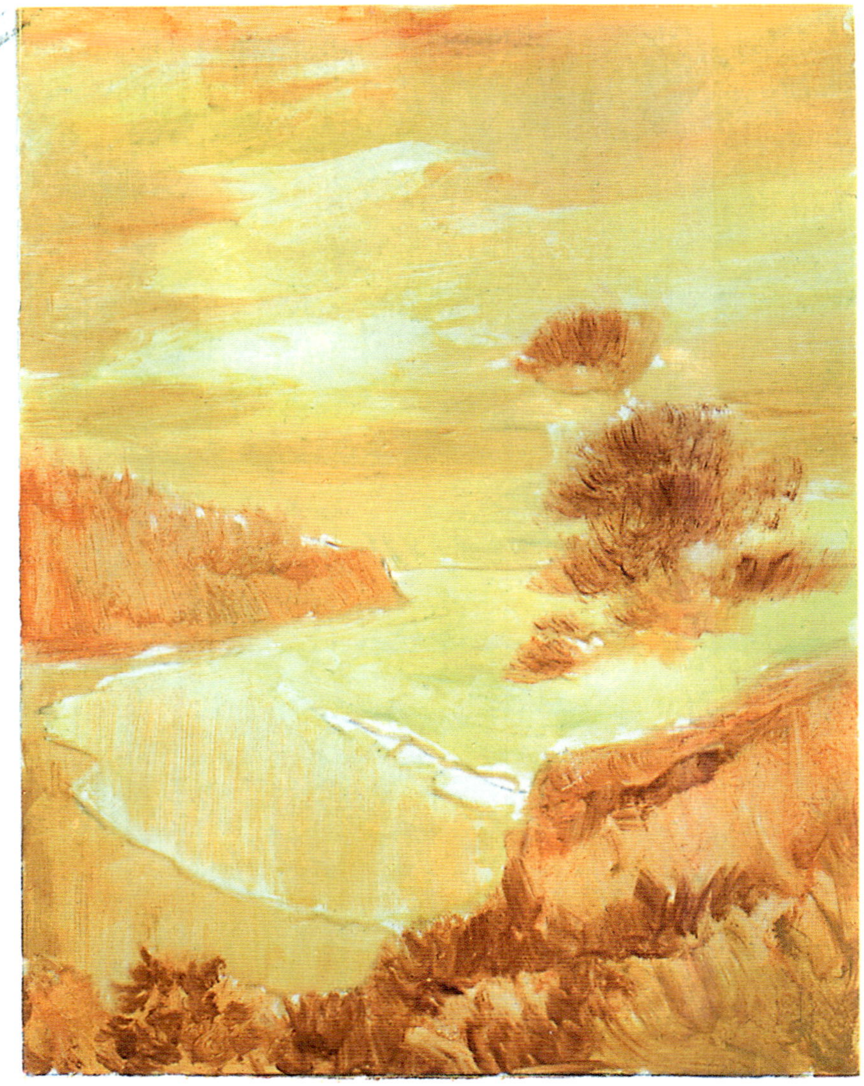

There is no blue in this sky. By adding Chrome Oxide Green on top of the gold, I have achieved the ILLUSION of blue, but have kept the painting in closer harmony than the use of blue would have achieved.

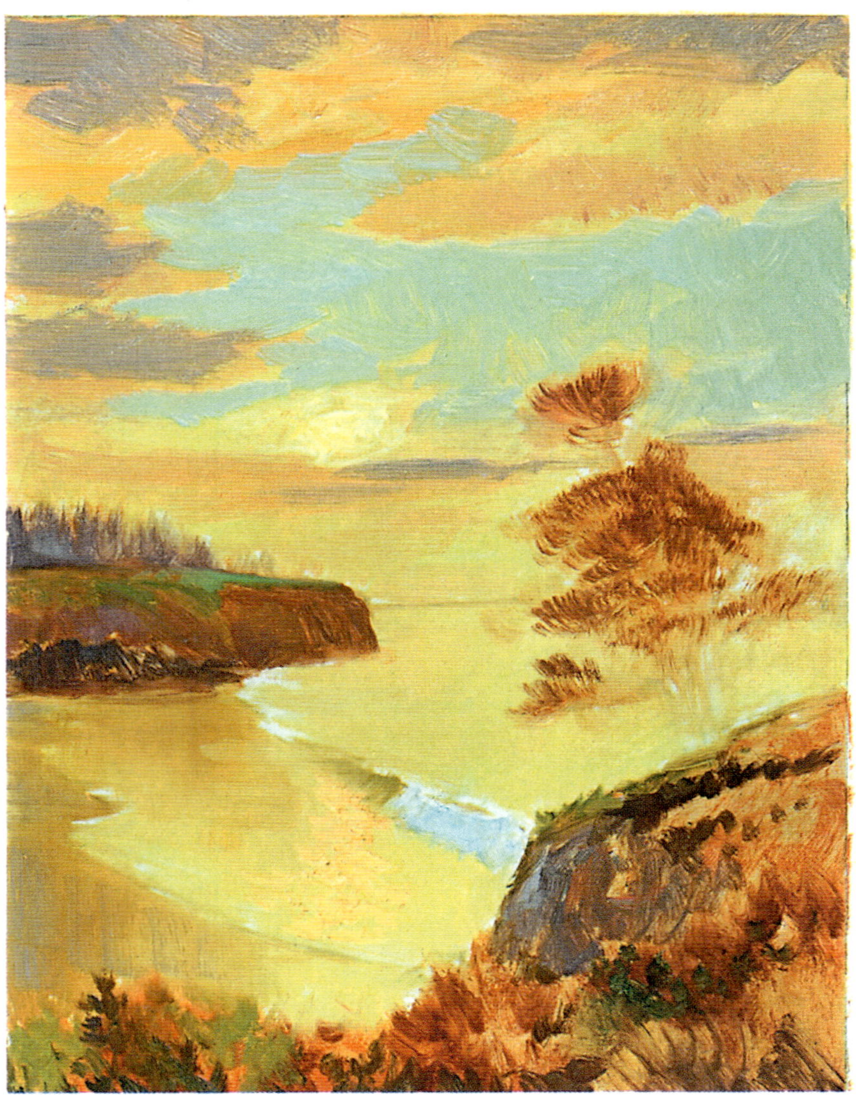

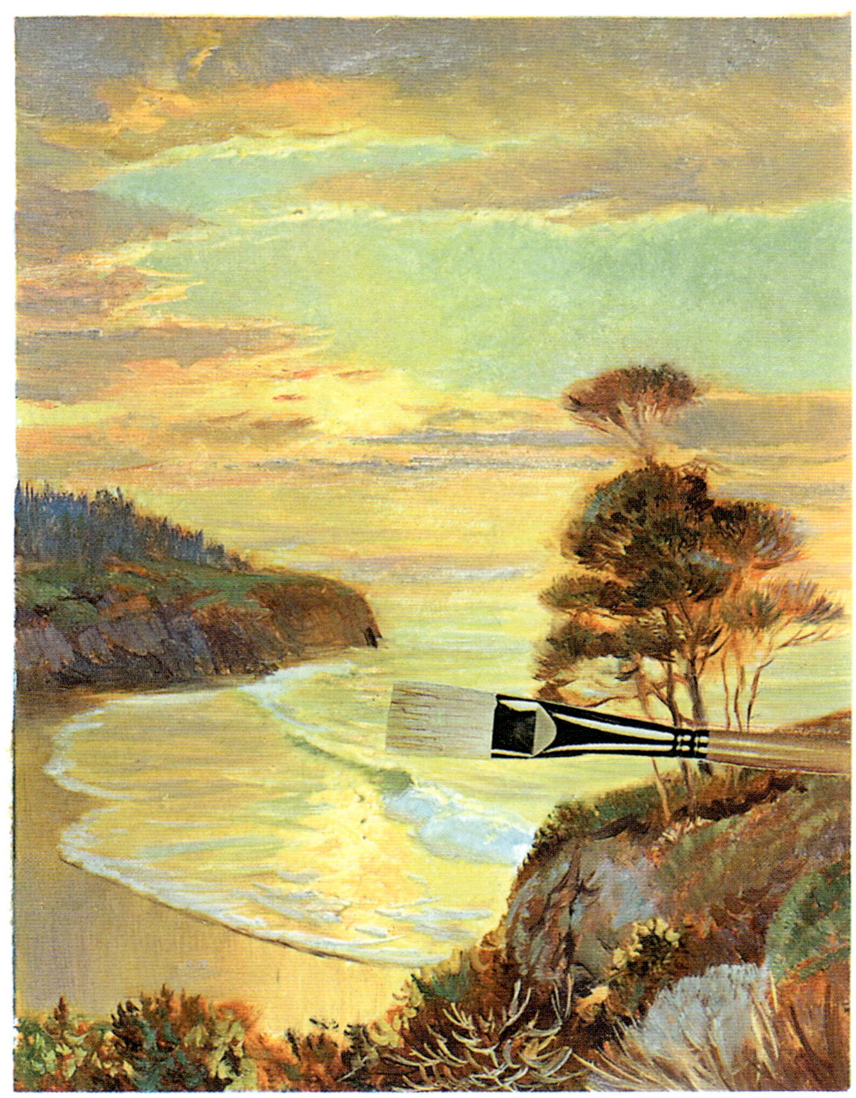

MENDOCINO MELODY. Backlit subjects are sometimes difficult, because we paint the subjects too dark. The darks are not black, but very colorful. Notice the halo-effect that occurs around a tree at sunset. Working from a photograph can often be deceptive, because the values that a camera picks up are wrong. The camera sees contrast, but the human eye sees half-tones. Look for the grays (the use of complementary colors) and vary these tones. The better the grays, the more intelligent the artist.

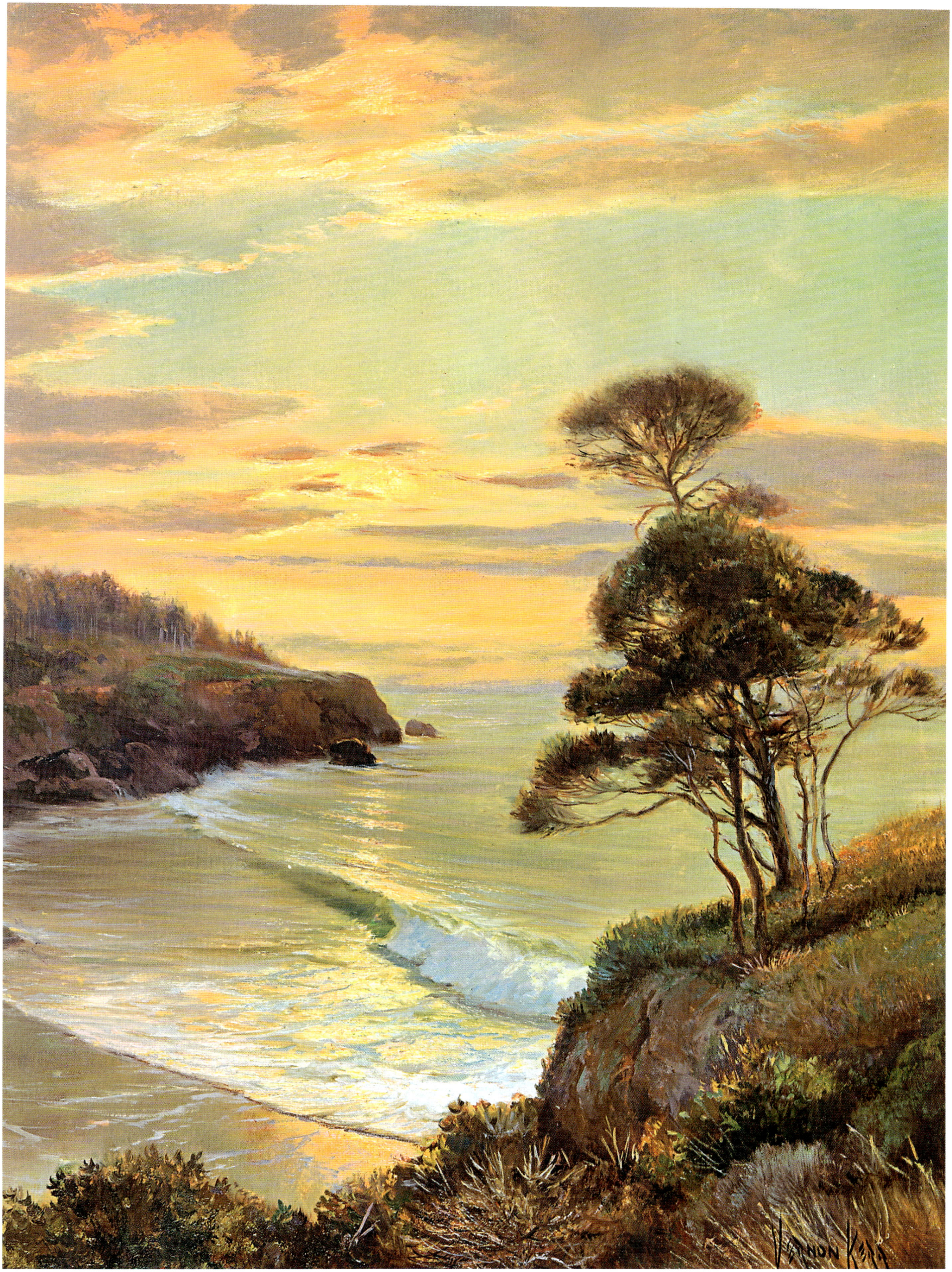

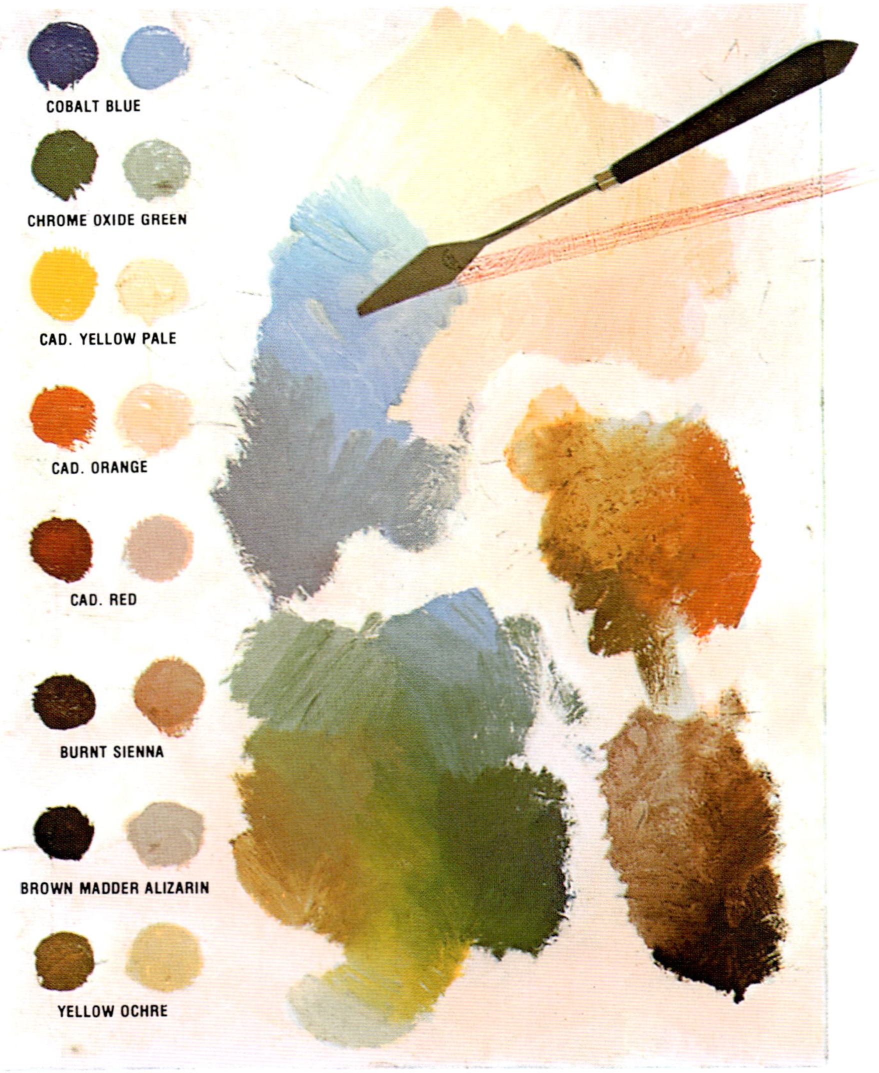

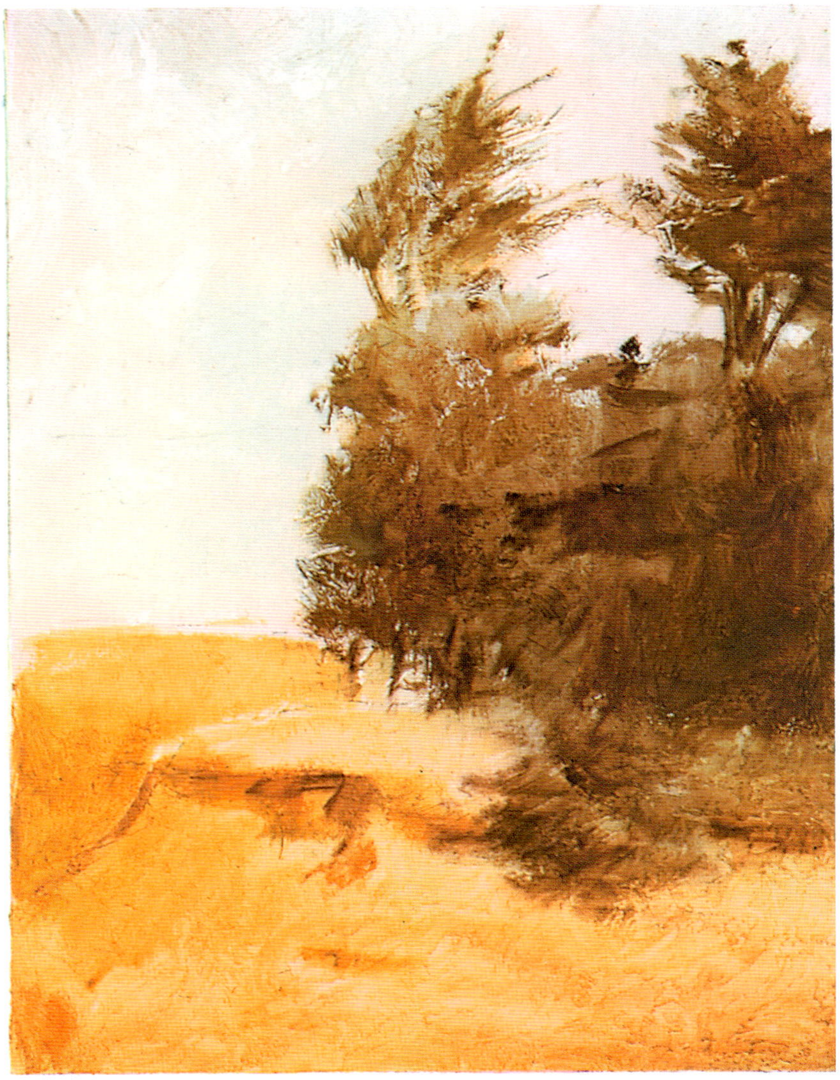

The key color to this painting is Brown Madder Alizarin, which is transparent and rich. Lay a wash of pure color and turpentine over each section of the picture, to eliminate all the white spots and establish pattern.

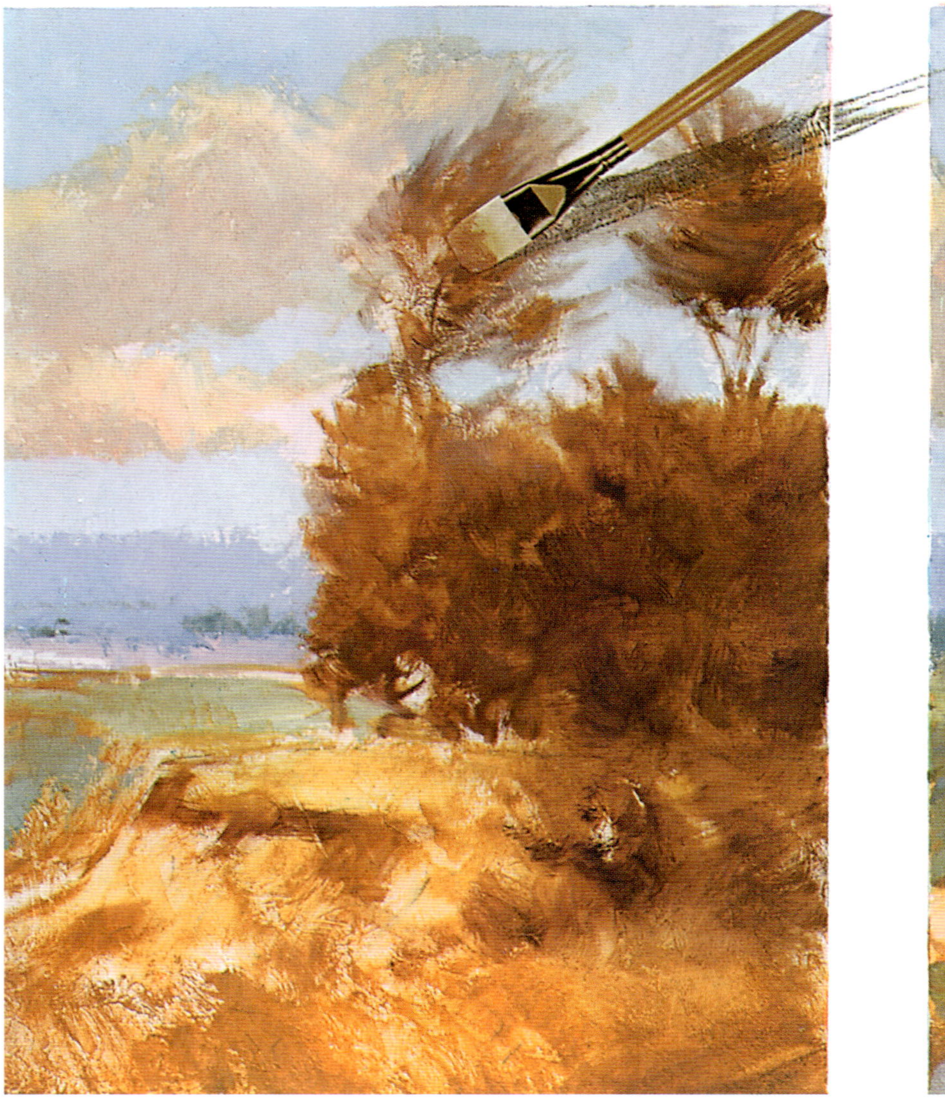

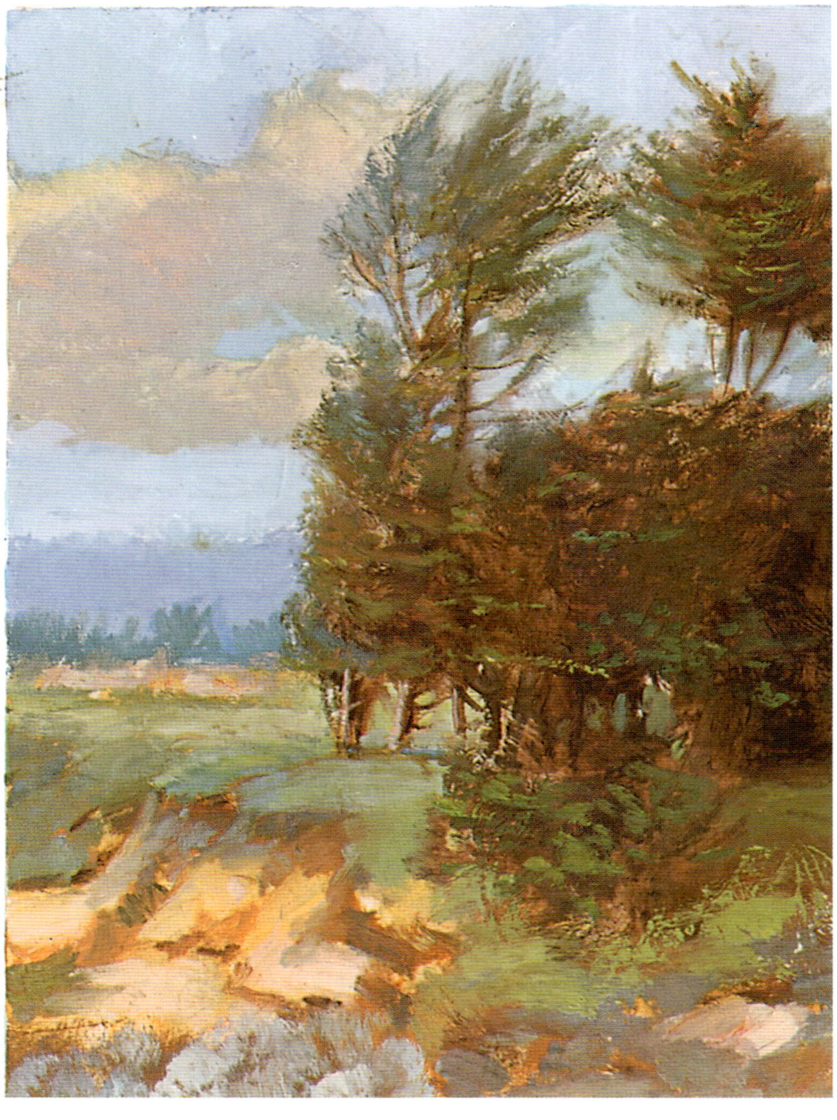

As you add more colors to the painting, try to establish the gesture of the wind-swept trees. On an overcast day, the colors will be muted and close in value. To create contrast, lay a premixed Yellow Ochre next to a premixed green. This creates a vibrancy without losing the overcast quality of the day.

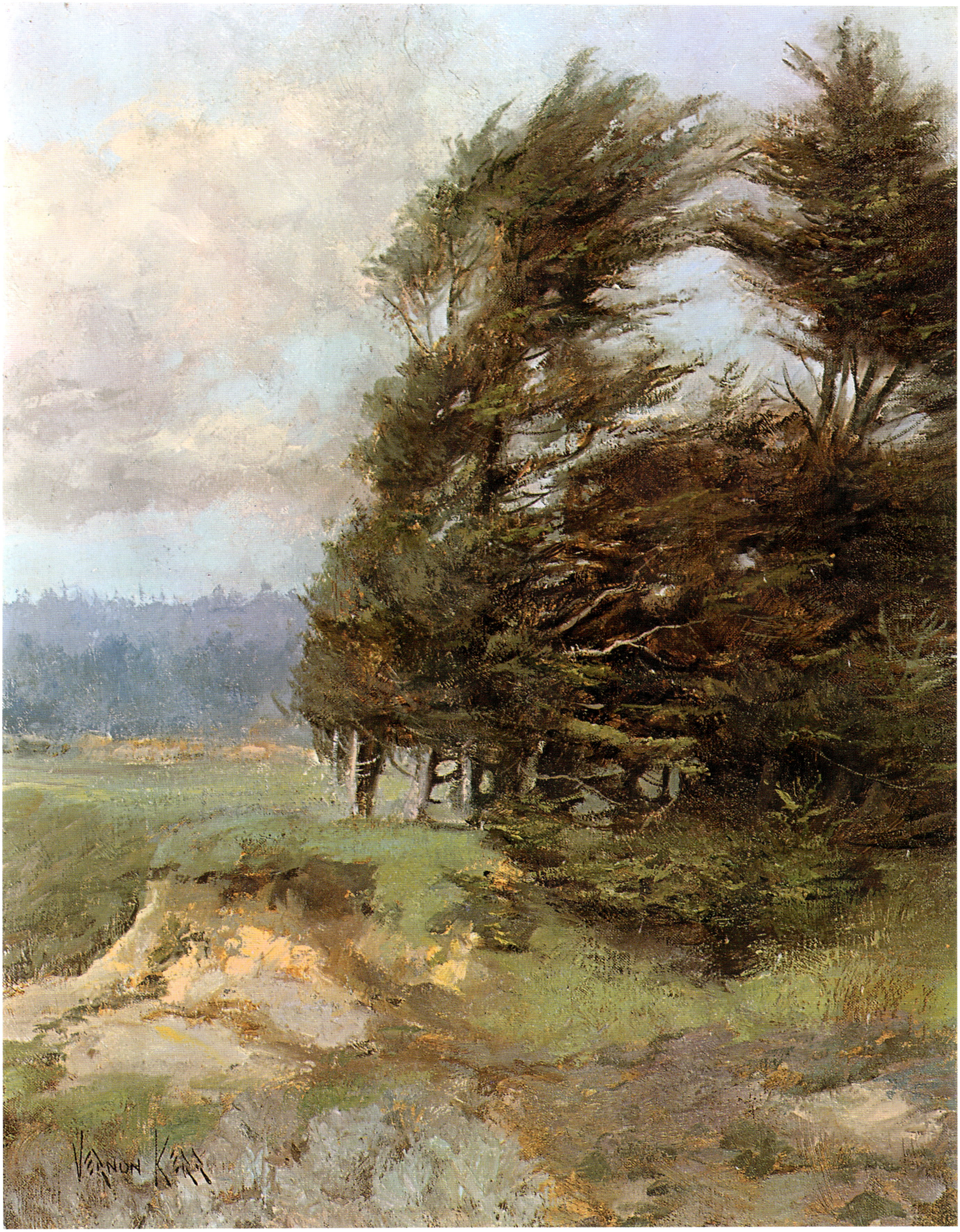

WIND SONG. This grove of cypress trees is on the bluff in front of my house. They have such dignity and character that I chose to share them with you. This painting was done on a textured canvas to achieve a more natural earthy feeling. Note that the strokes are kept loose and the edges soft, which adds to the wind-blown feeling that is felt at the edge of a bluff.

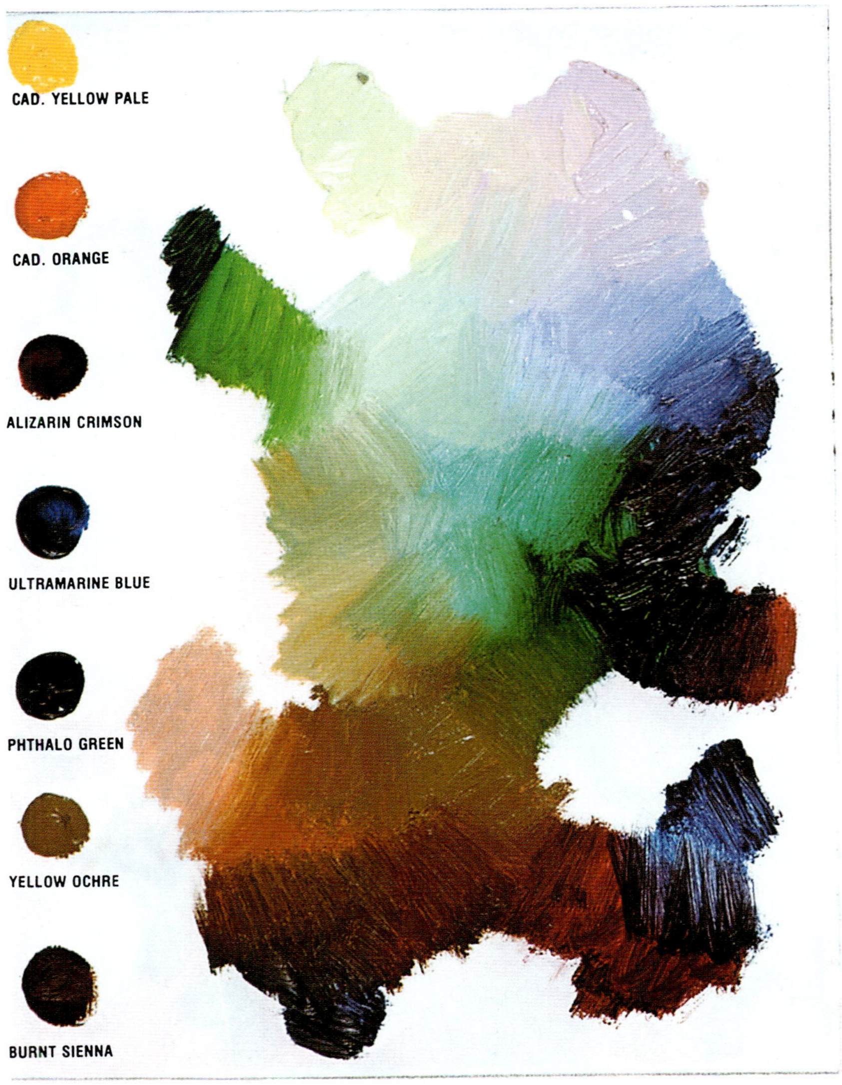

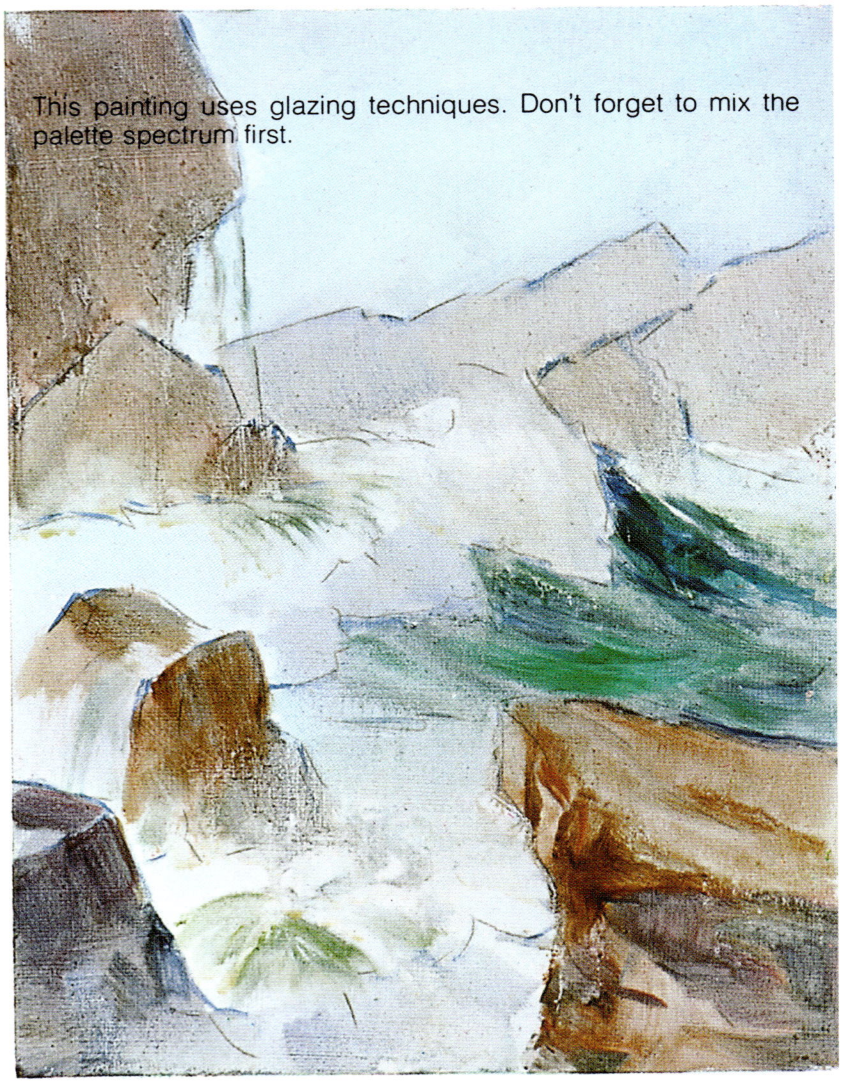

This painting uses glazing techniques. Don't forget to mix the palette spectrum first.

On a gesso board, use the glazing medium and glaze the colors thinly (pure colors only). NO TURP WASH!

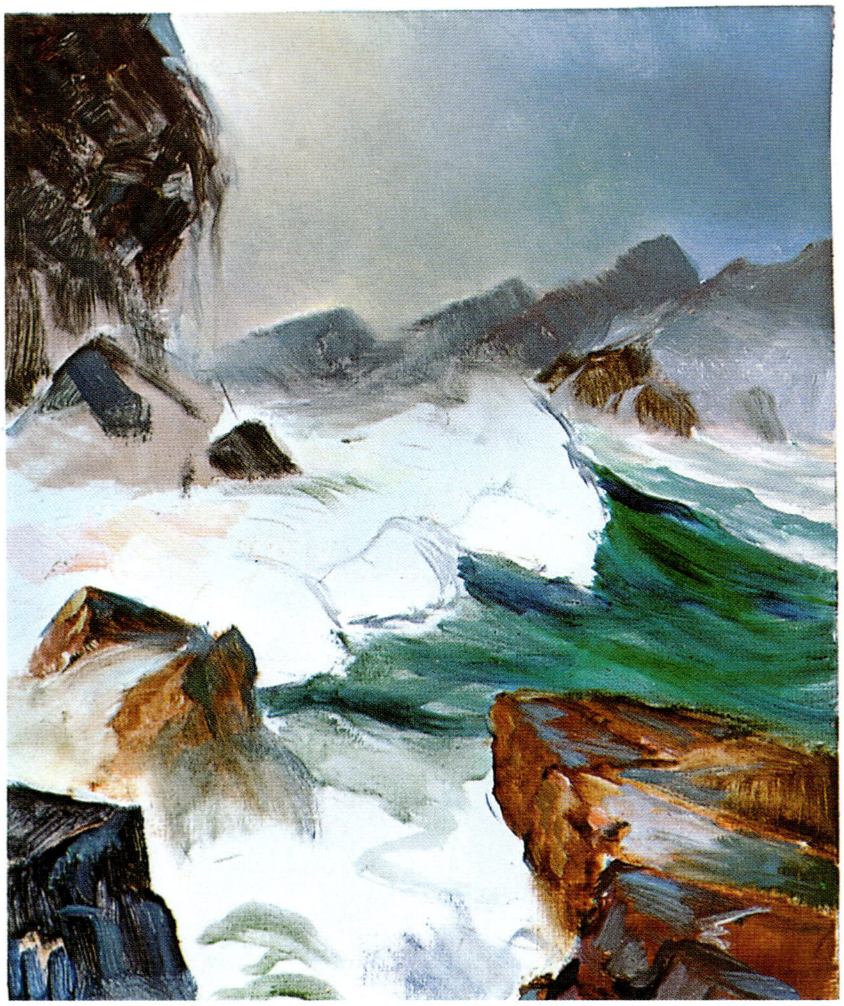

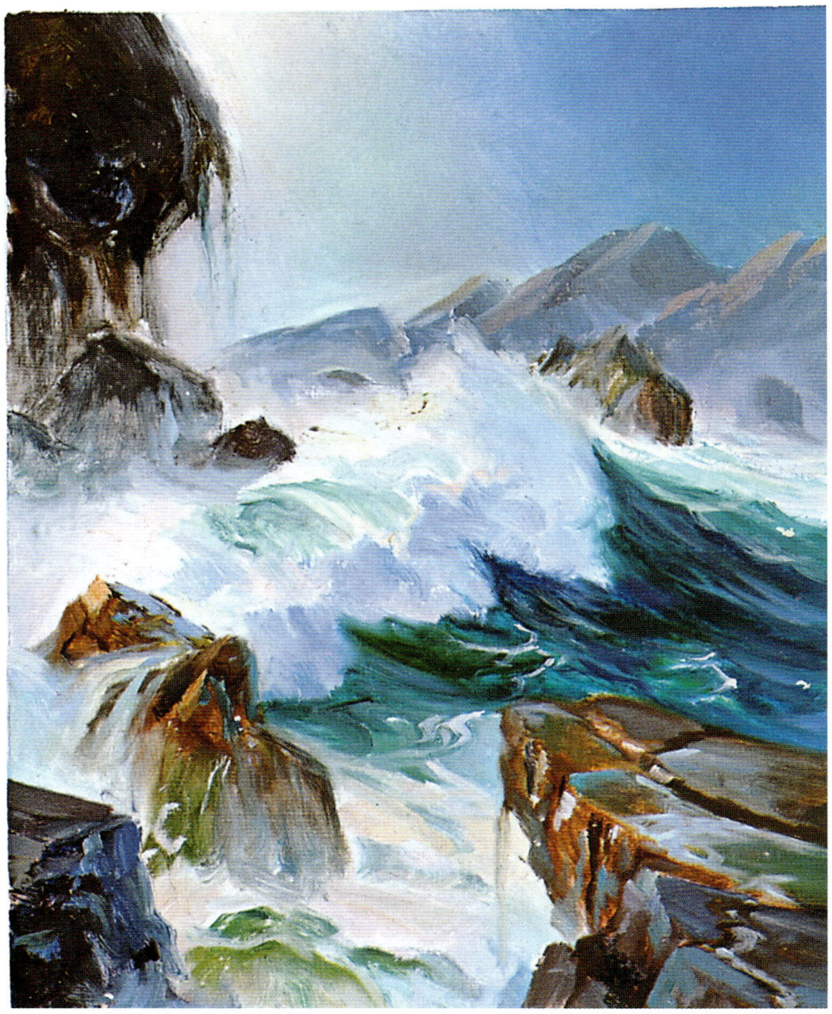

THE STORM KING. Note that the strength of this painting is achieved by the extreme contrasts of complementary colors, darks and lights and soft and hard edges. These are the tools of the artist to give the paintings VITALITY. Be sure to establish darks first in the underpainting. Use premixes for the sky, far cliffs, and rock at top left. Paint the dark water, but let the undercolor show through. For the foam use the pastel premixes and roll the paint on thickly, but don't blend totally—this will keep the lights luminous and beautiful. Carefully paint the shadowed part of the wave. Build up the rocks gradually, using very little opaque color. Instead use rich pigment, then later add the premix colors. The cracks of the rocks are rich and warm.

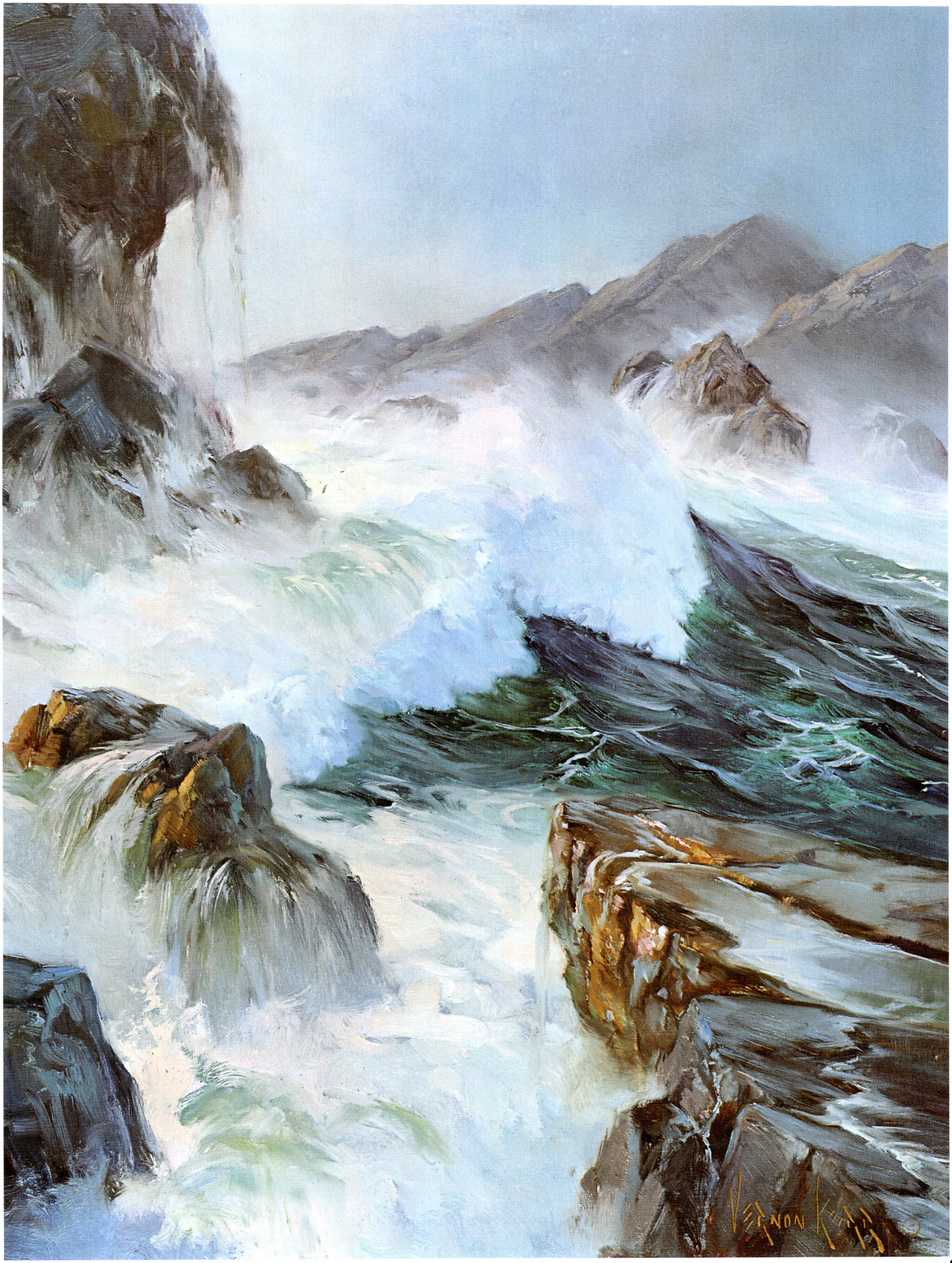

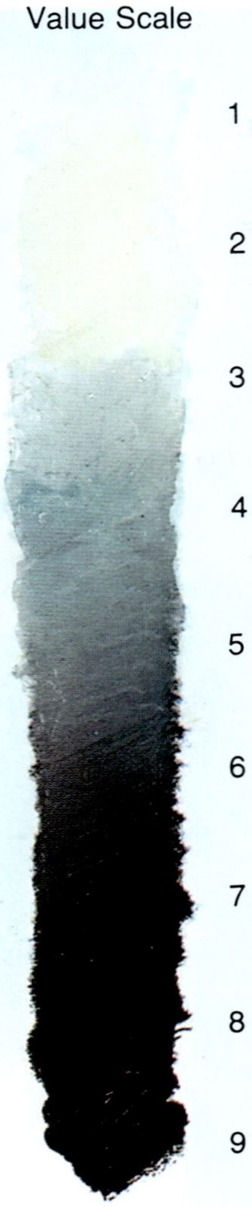

Make a Value Scale and keep it near your canvas. Put a Value Guide on your outdoor easel. The #5 Value is a key to traditional painting and is used as a reference point.

Value Guide for Outdoors

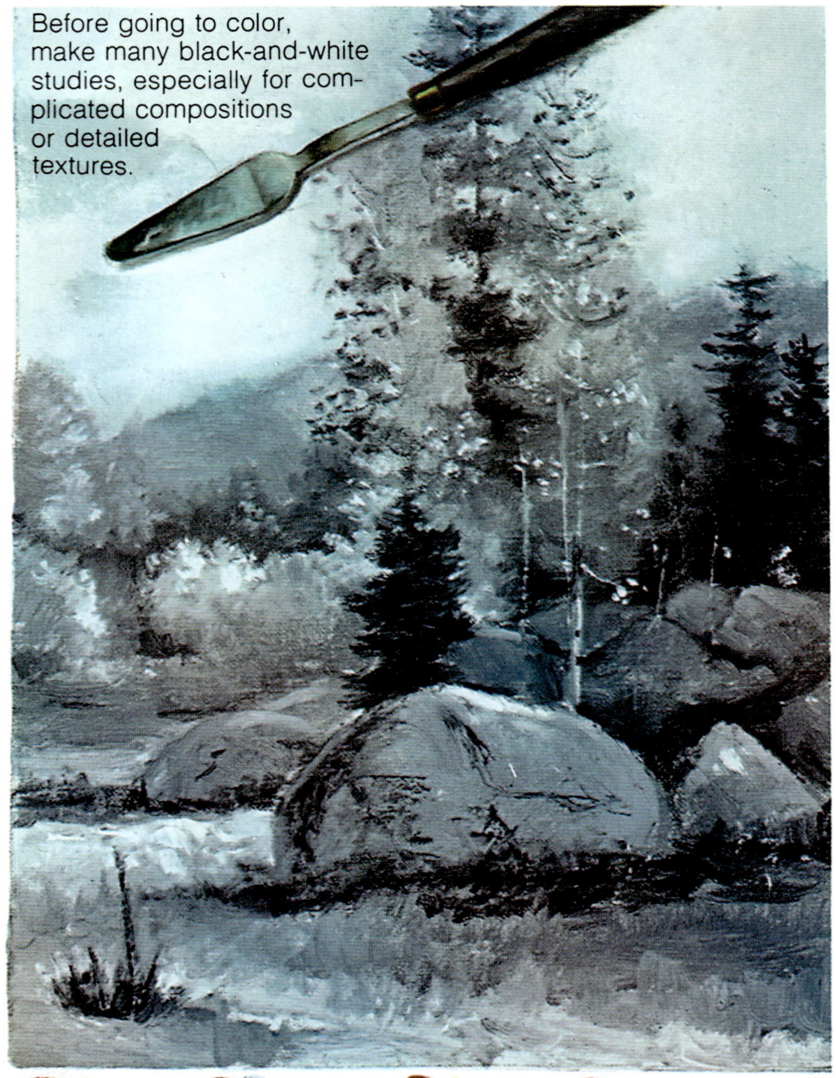

Before going to color, make many black-and-white studies, especially for complicated compositions or detailed textures.

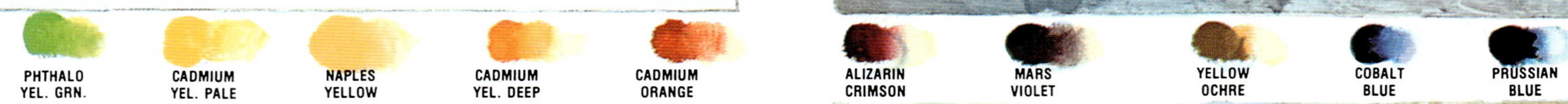

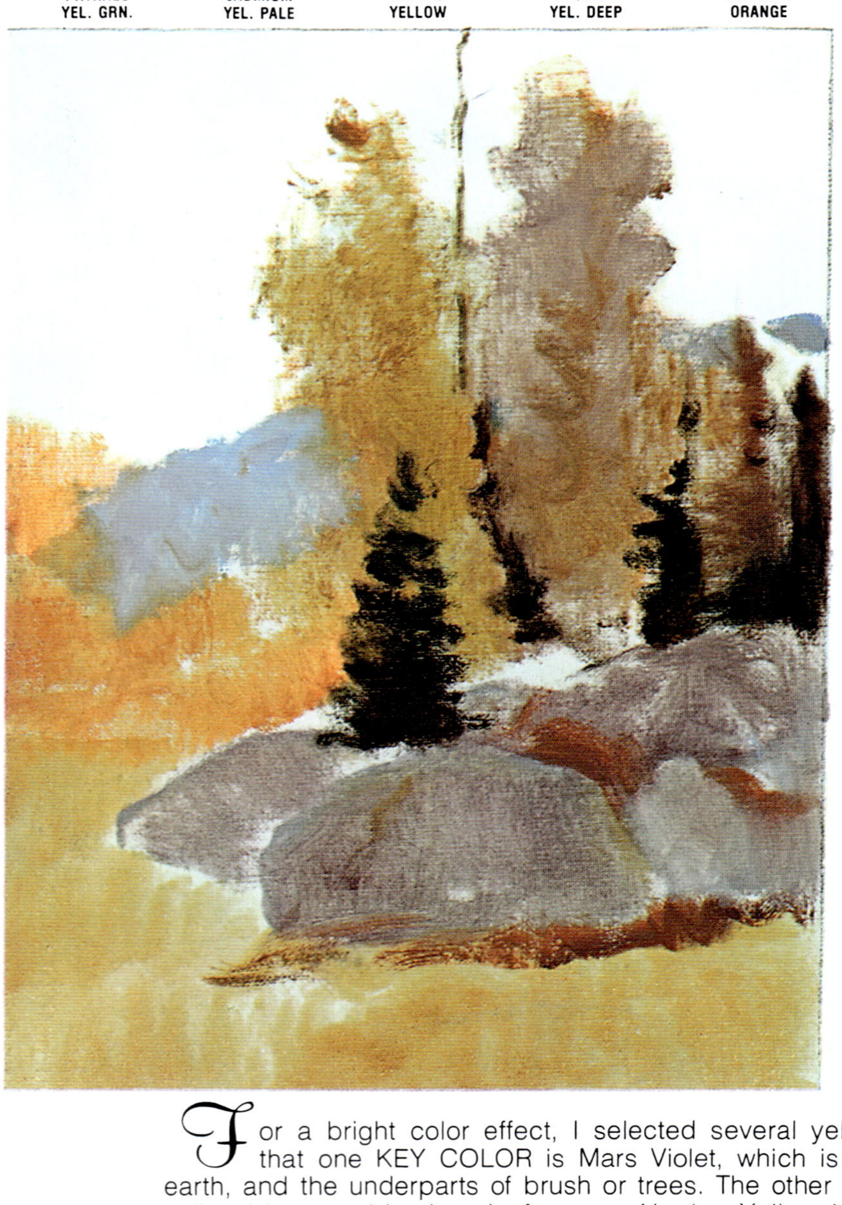

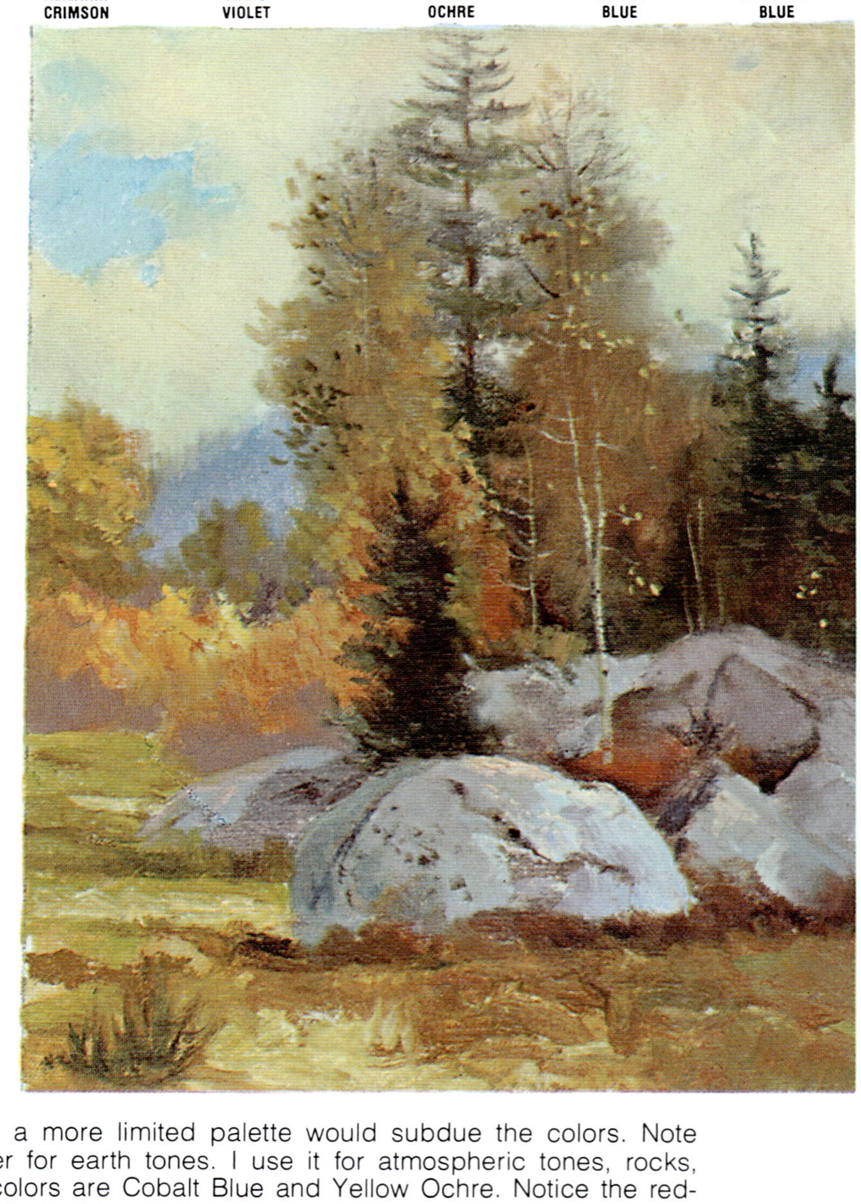

For a bright color effect, I selected several yellows; a more limited palette would subdue the colors. Note that one KEY COLOR is Mars Violet, which is super for earth tones. I use it for atmospheric tones, rocks, earth, and the underparts of brush or trees. The other key colors are Cobalt Blue and Yellow Ochre. Notice the red-yellow-blue combination. I often use Naples Yellow instead of white to lighten color combinations, because it is opaque and saves mixing time. I've discovered that the rich darks for close-up pines can be made from Orange and Prussian Blue. Of course, add other colors when necessary.

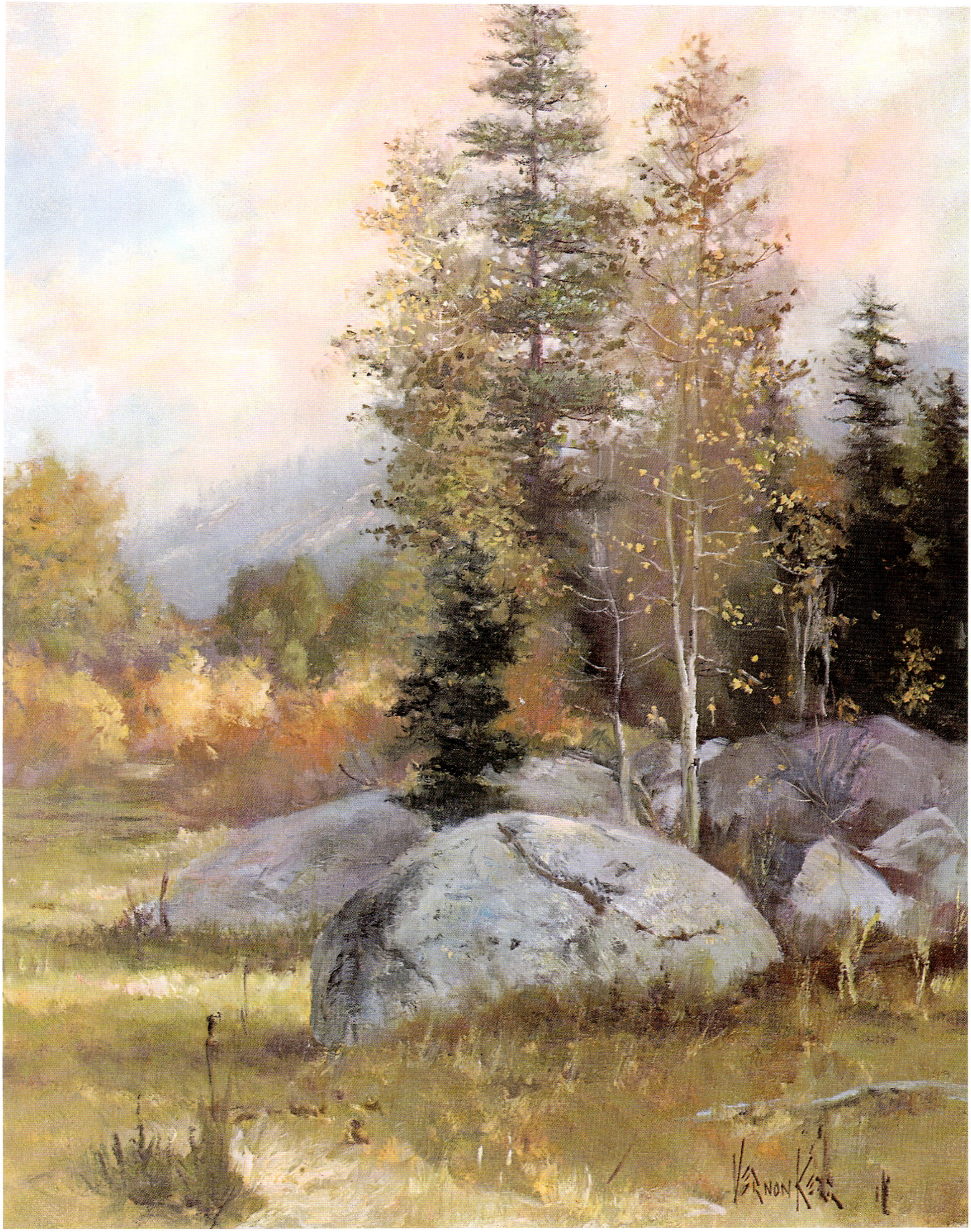

SURRENDER TO FALL. This is an outdoor sketch near Lake Tahoe, California, and a good exercise in textures. I chose a bright, crisp morning, with the light skipping across the trees, grass, and rocks. I used a smooth canvas. With bristle brushes, underpaint the general parts first. With a knife, smooth and blend the sky, then build up the textures of the rocks. Pull the background together to soften the edges. Paint the skyholes in the trees darker in value than the sky, or you will have little dots staring at you. When the painting is dry, you can add the final details, such as the yellow leaves and grasses.

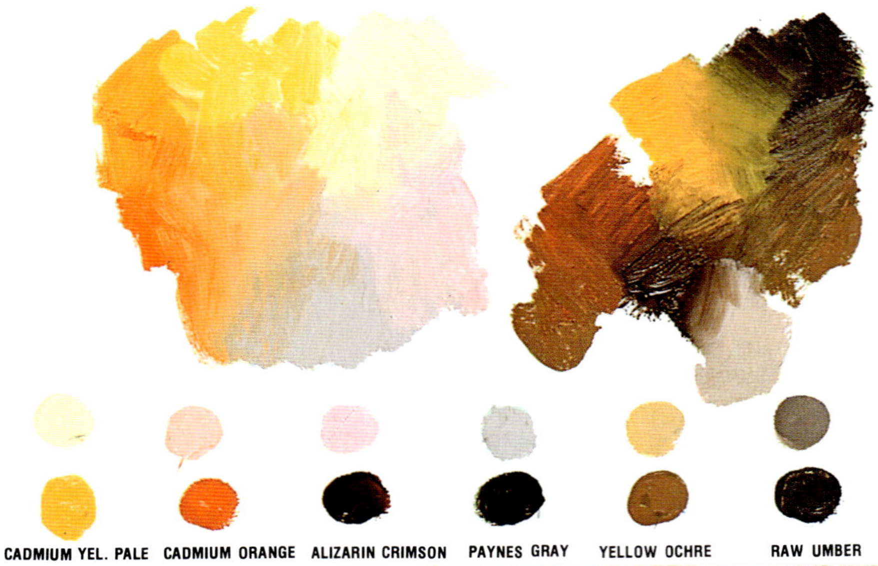

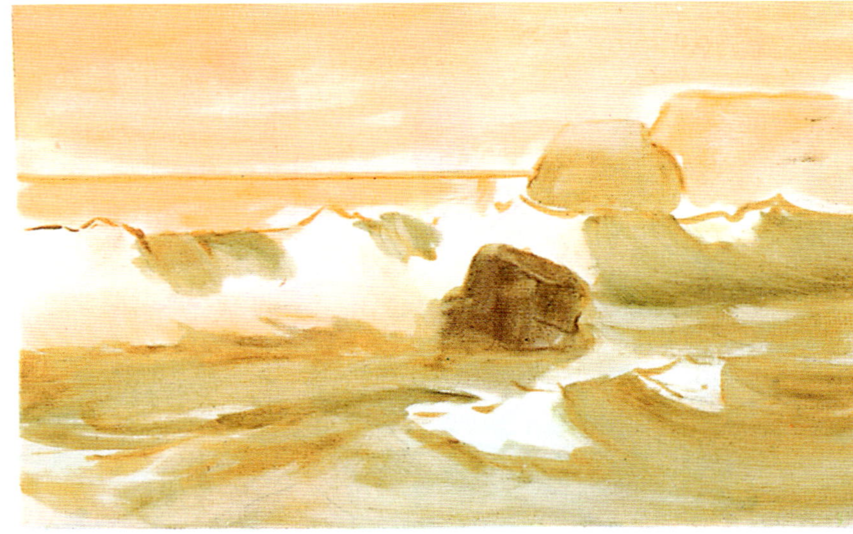

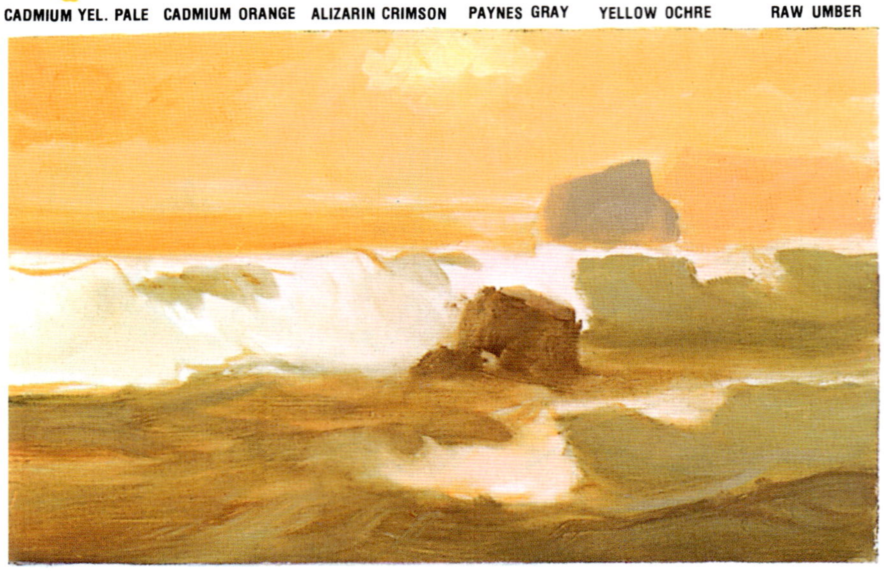

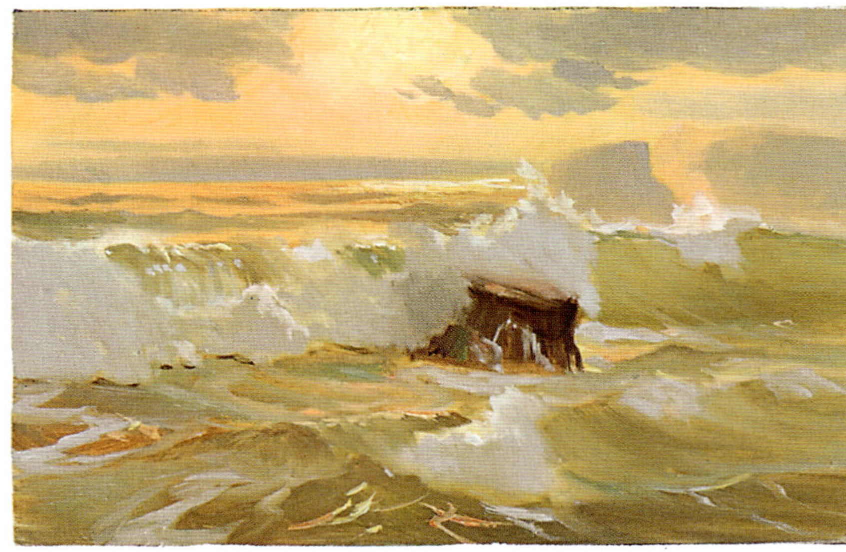

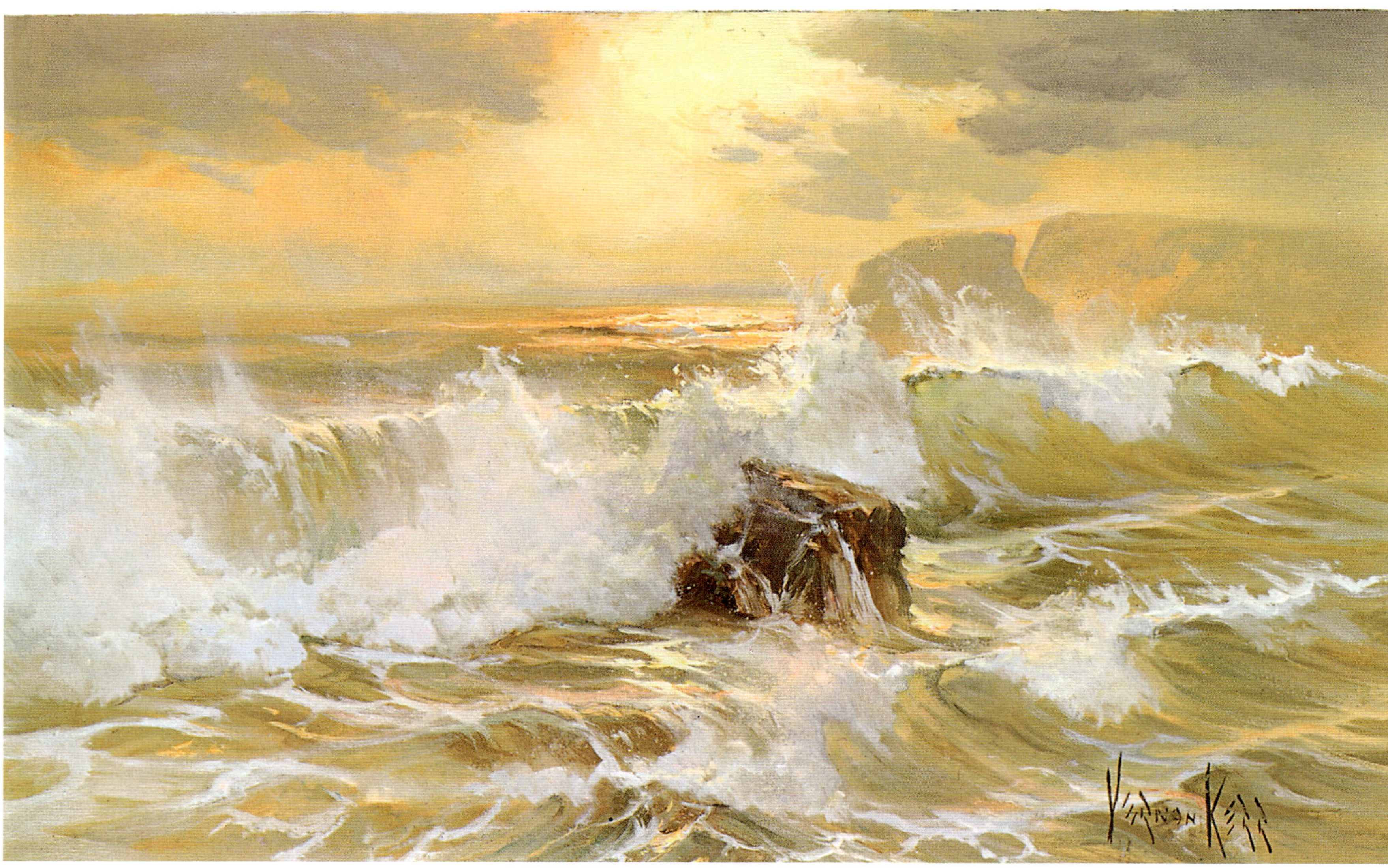

CITRON SUNSET. When painting a yellow-gold sunset, we can omit the use of blue, because overmixing blue can cause the yellows to be dull. Instead we can give the ILLUSION of blue. This is called color optics. Burnt Umber plus White appears to be lavender, and Paynes Gray plus White looks blue. In this picture, the colors are primarily mixed on the canvas, allowing the accidental color effects from the under-painting to create luminosity.

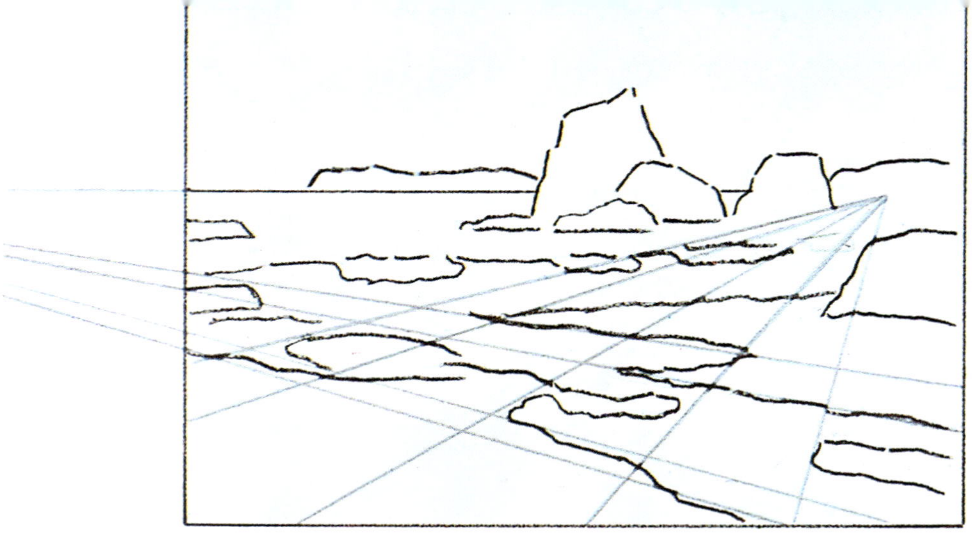

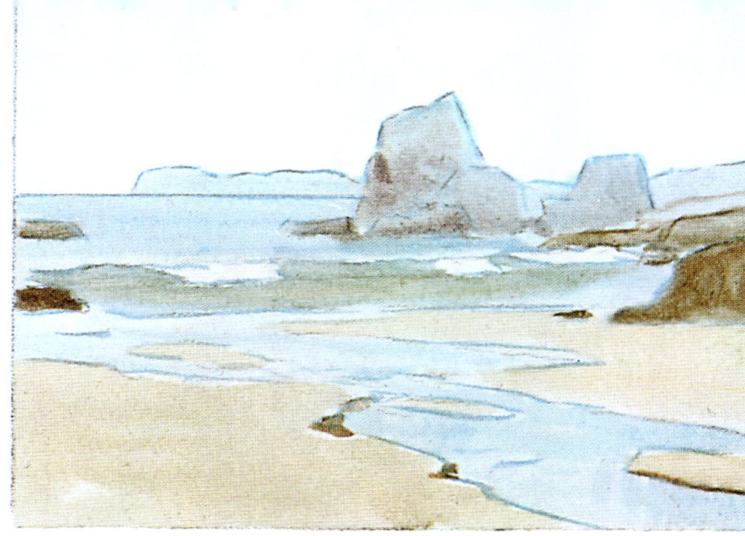

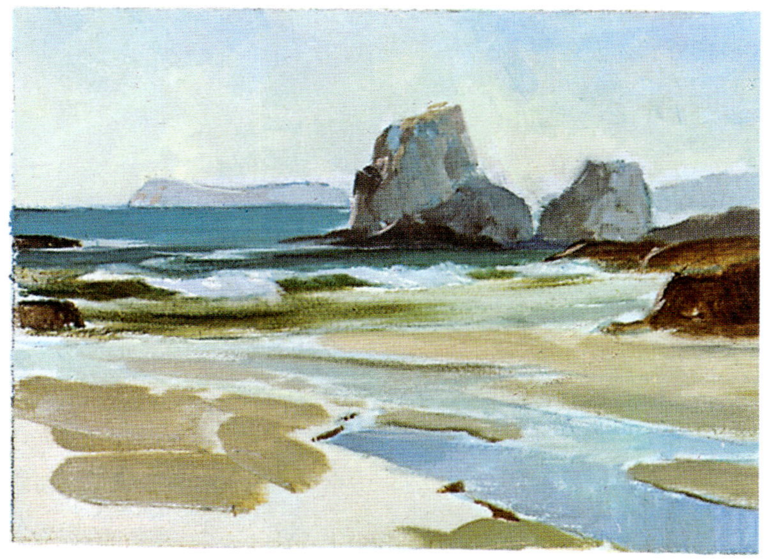

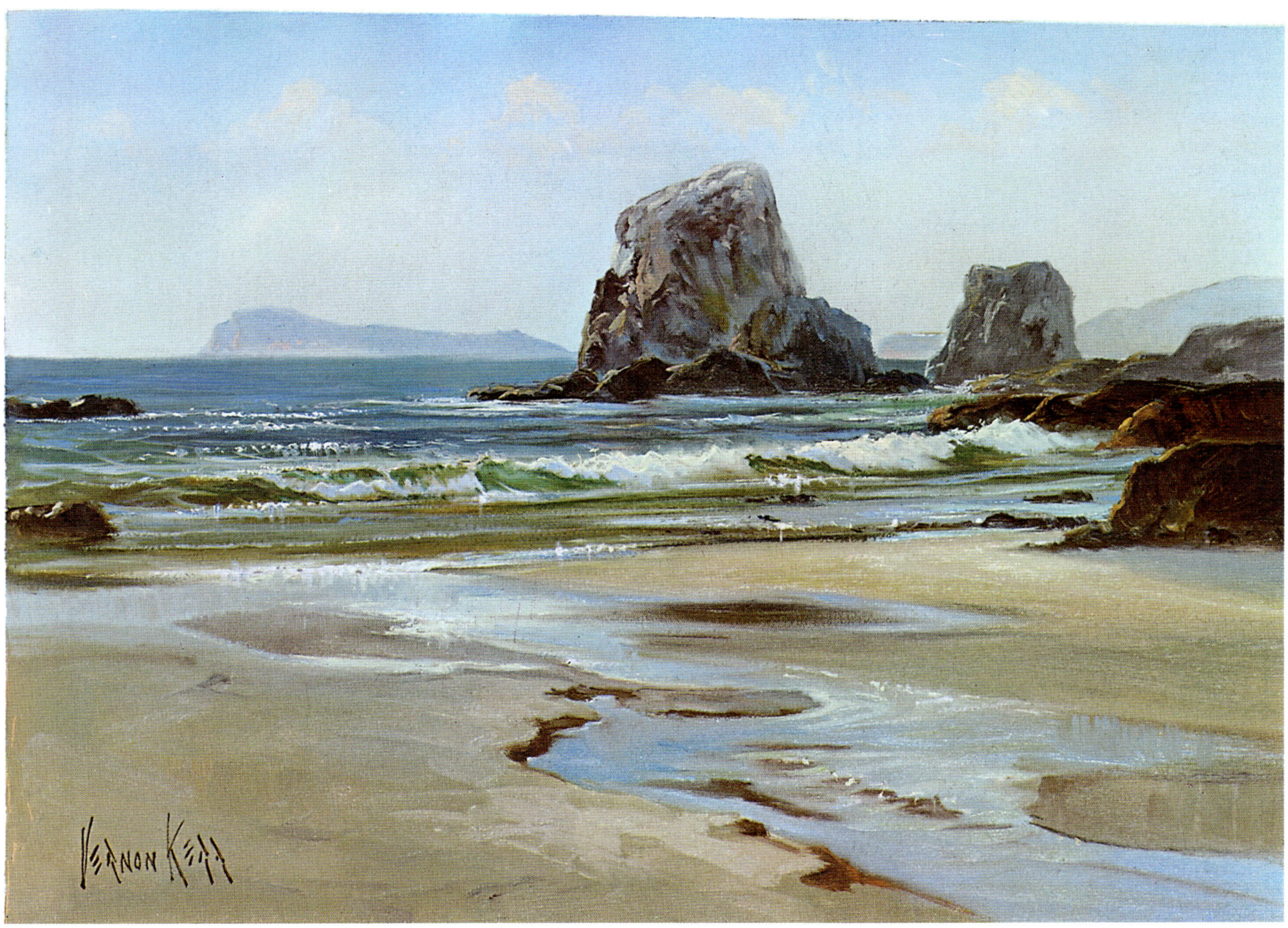

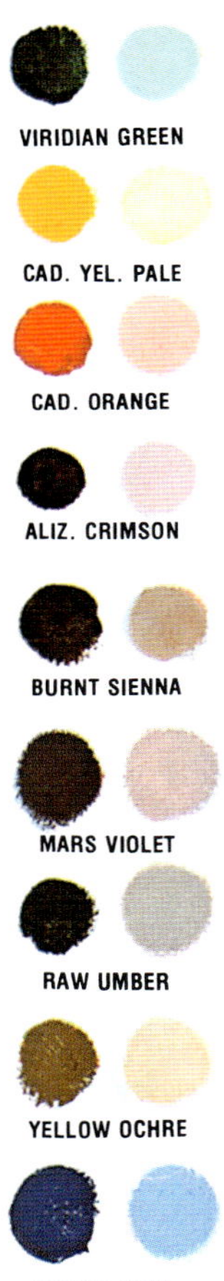

ANCHOR BAY. Up to this point I haven't mentioned perspective. Walter Foster has a fine book on the subject. Locate the vanishing points! Make a careful drawing, or a black-and-white painting first. Establish your color and value relationships by first spotting in the darkest darks and the lightest lights. Cover the largest areas. Paint the middle area (the water and rocks), then the sky, and leave the beach until last. A tip about painting sand: Mix all the leftover colors of your palette spectrum together and use it in your sand color. This ties together all the colors in the painting.

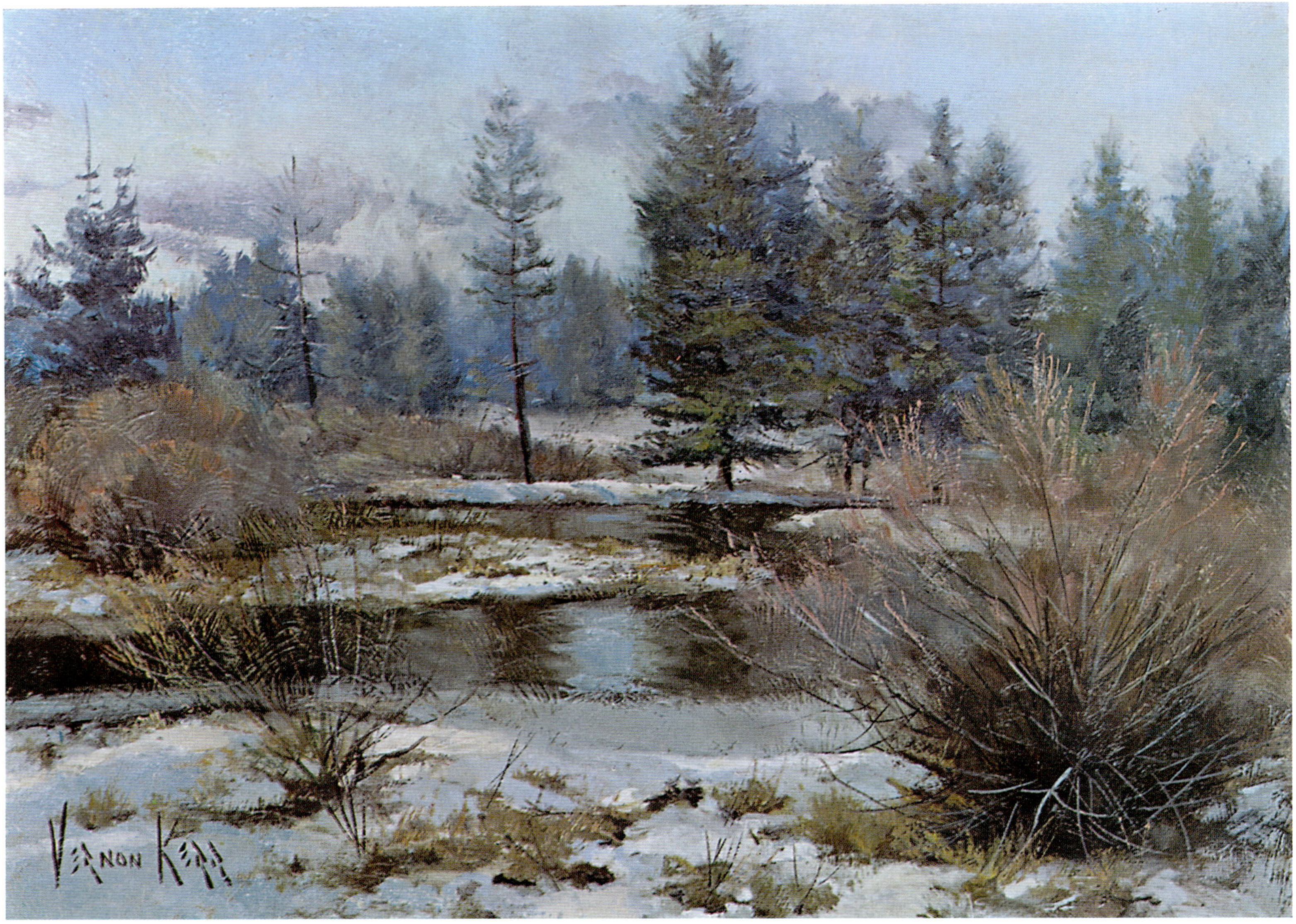

LAPINE SNOW.
These are two 12x16 sketches done on location in Lapine, Central Oregon. I tried to vary the composition, especially in the bushes, and to show that the ground does not have to be completely covered with snow to be effective. Don't you agree that the red bushes make an intriguing contrast?

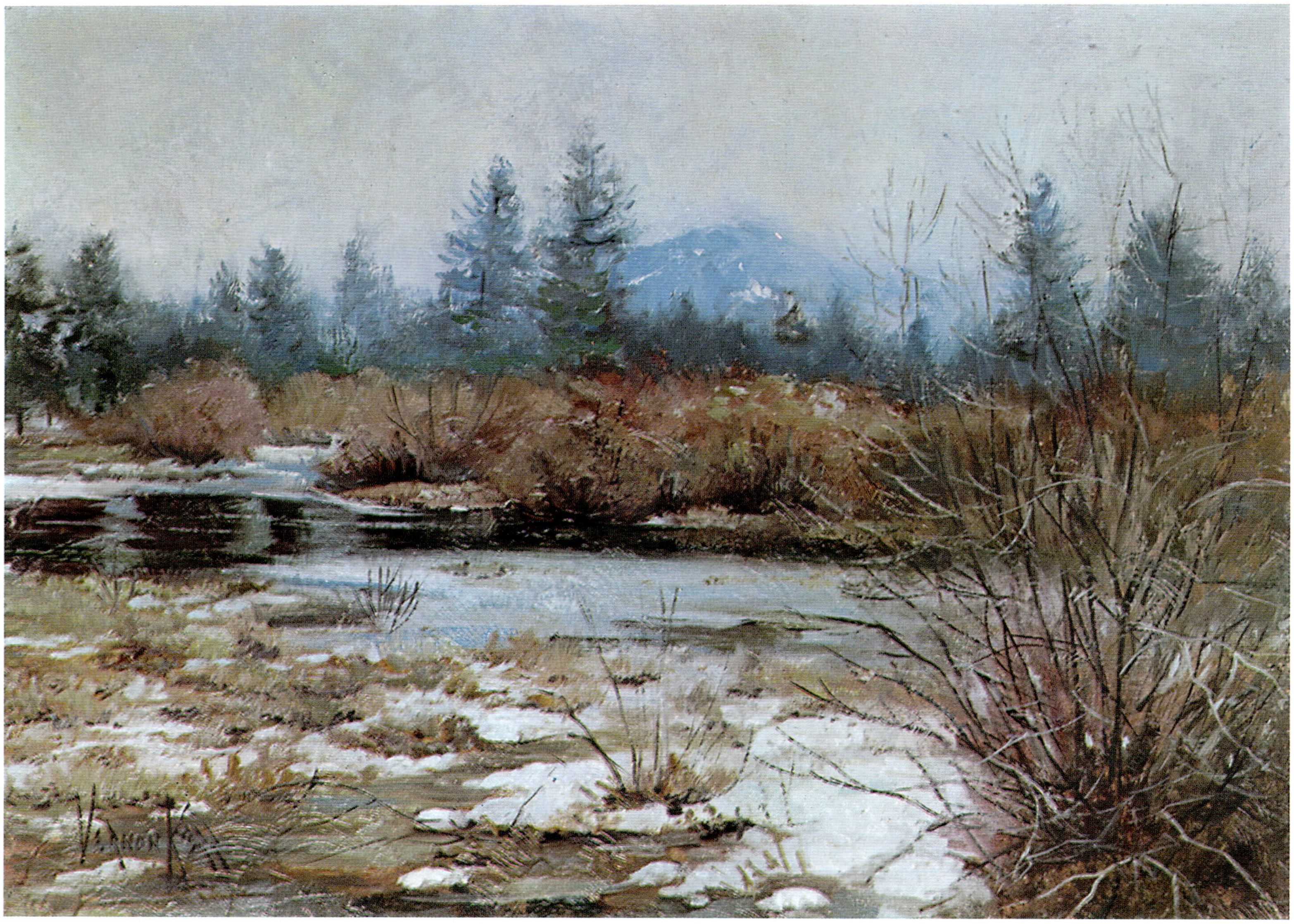

SNOW STUDIES. I cannot stress too much the importance of making studies, all kinds of studies. My studio shelves are lined with oil sketches of different subjects in both monotone and color. The bark of a tree, for instance, is a fascinating balance of textures and colors. Note the warm lights on the sunny side, and the cool reflected lights on the shady side of the trunk. When snow piles against a tree trunk, it sends fingers up the grooves of the trunk, and it spreads out at the base to blend with the snow on the ground.

Snow colors do not have to be white with blue shadows! Glowing snow has all colors in it. Notice the shades of yellow, and lavender, and pink, and green. Don't forget to add the reflected lights. In the stream picture, notice the lights the snow picks up from the water beneath it.

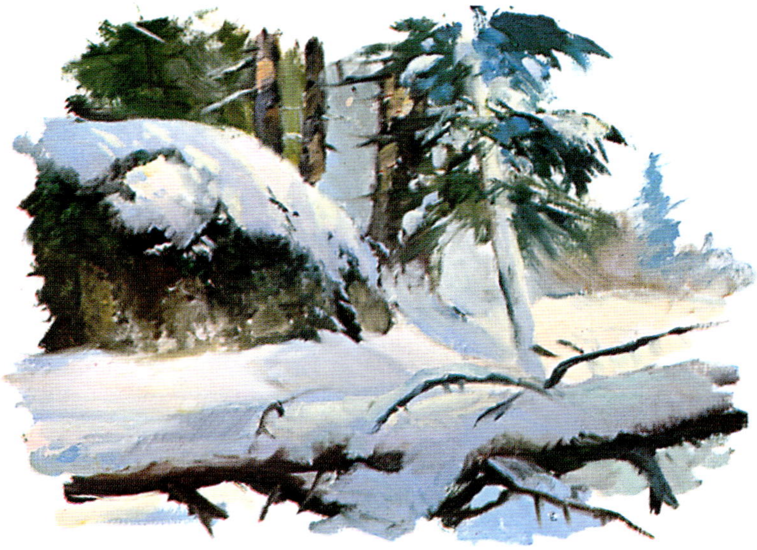

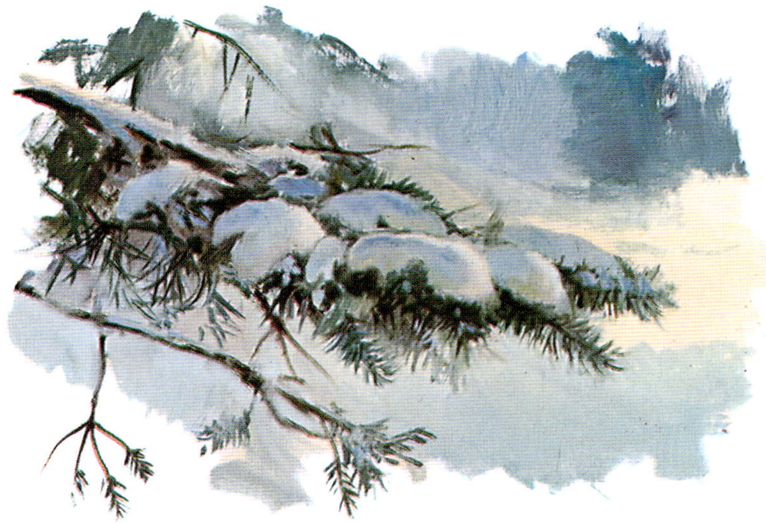

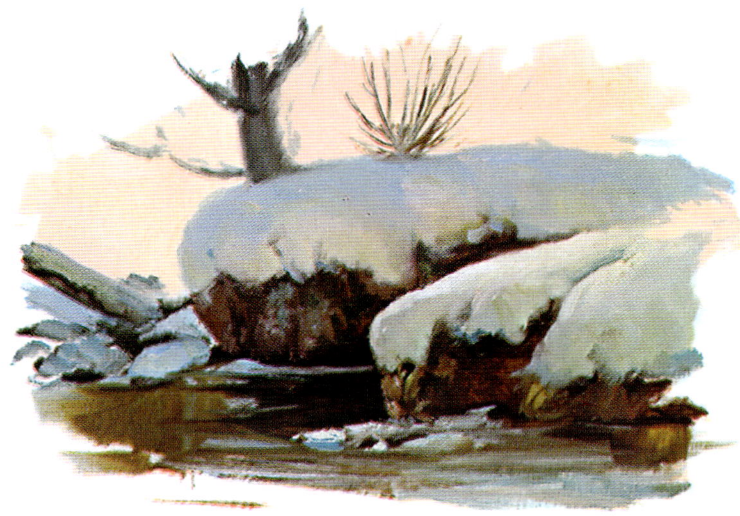

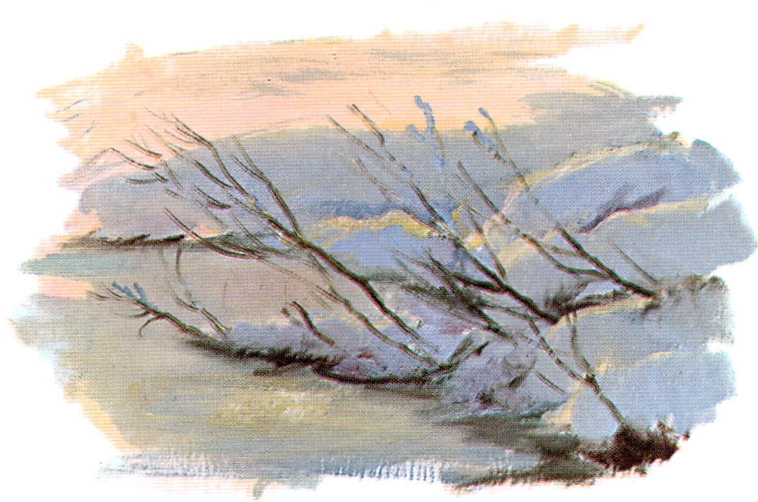

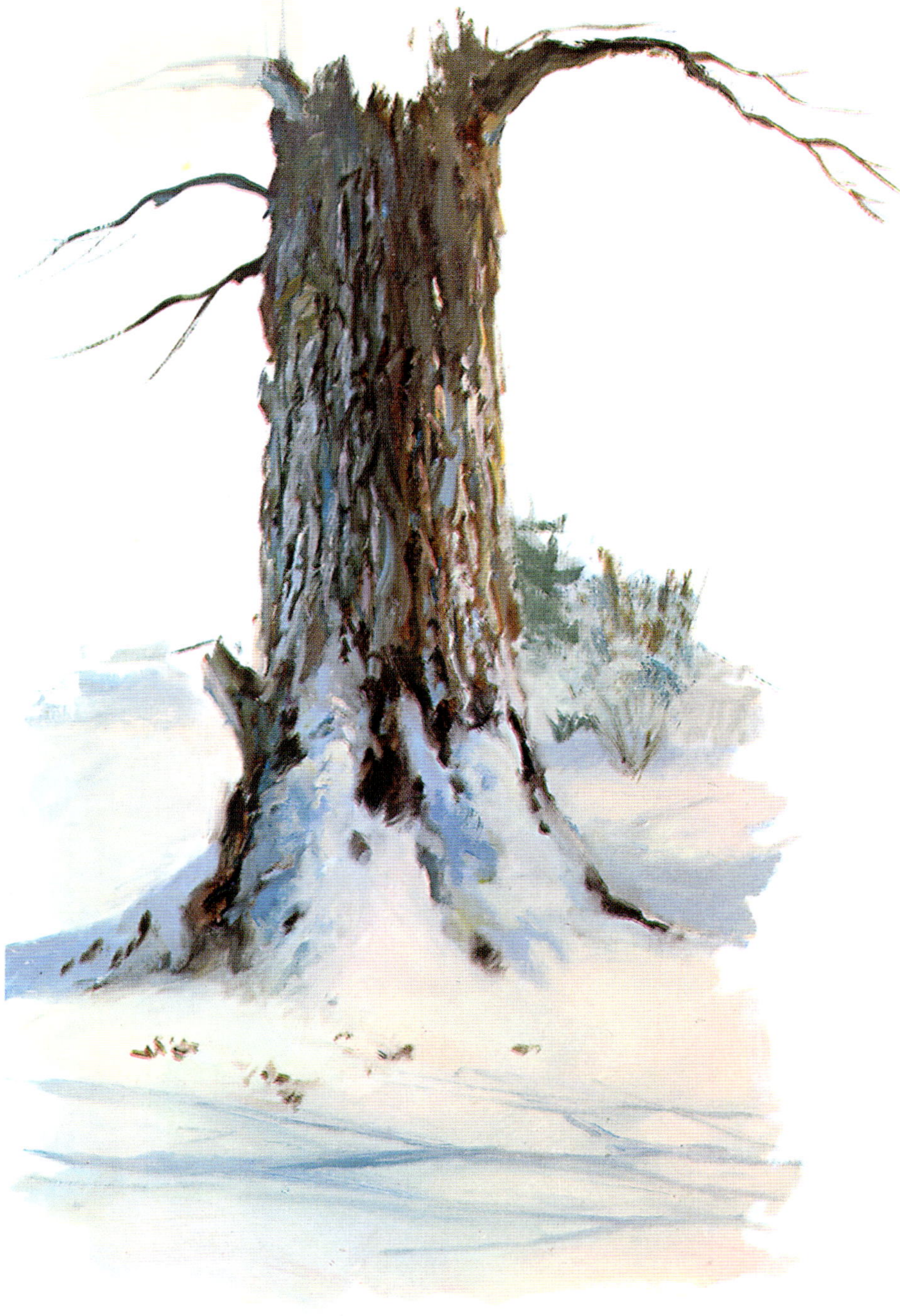

SPECTRUM SKIES. When I first started painting as a child, I used to climb on the rooftop to paint skies. Skies are important: they often make up ⅓ of a painting. I feel that if you can paint good skies, it forces you to paint the other elements just as well. These sketches show that skies can be created from almost any color to achieve different effects. Try to memorize cloud formations, and know the various clouds for various conditions. Collect photos for reference.

Experiment with different shades of blue; I've found that Cobalt Blue makes a good afternoon sky color. Theoretically, you can paint any picture with a basic red, yellow, and blue, BUT I use pre-tubed color (such as Naples Yellow or Cadmium Orange) to create clean color and to save mixing.

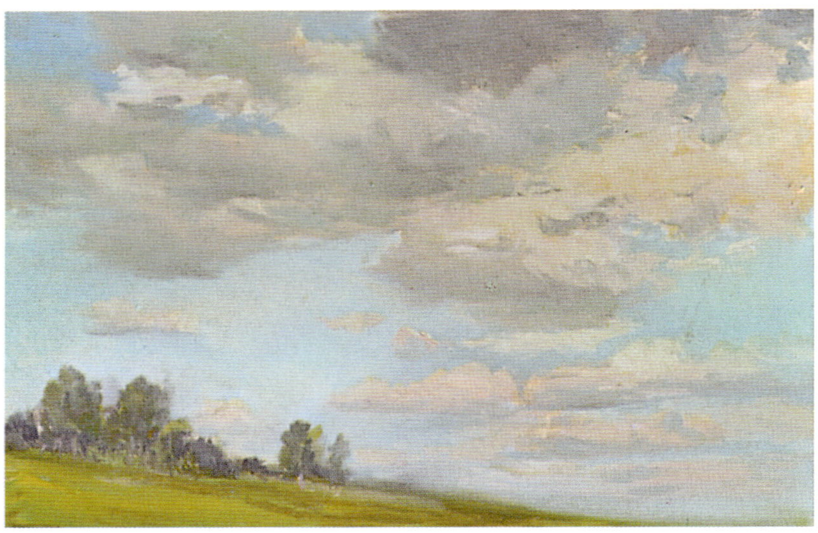

1. Cadmium Yellow Pale, Yellow Ochre, Alizarin Crimson, Cobalt Blue.

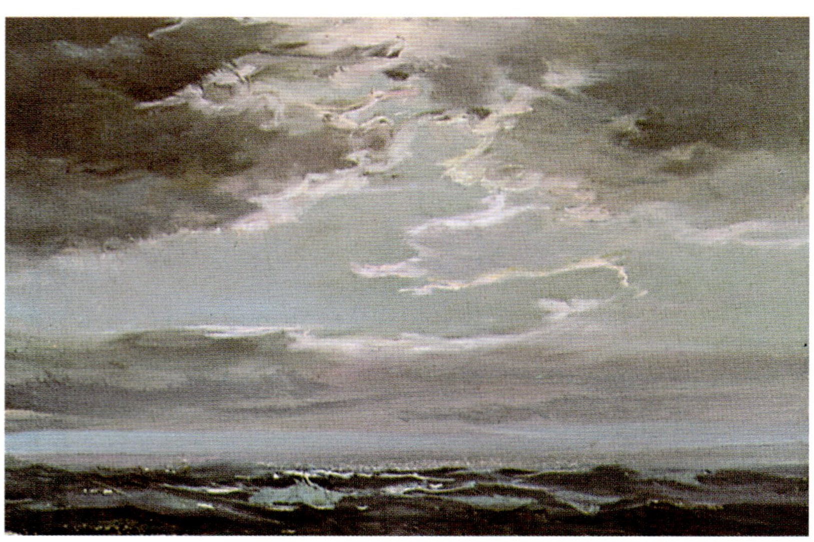

2. Cadmium Yellow Pale, Alizarin Crimson, Burnt Sienna, Prussian Blue.

3. Cadmium Yellow Pale, Cadmium Red, Viridian Green, Cobalt Blue.

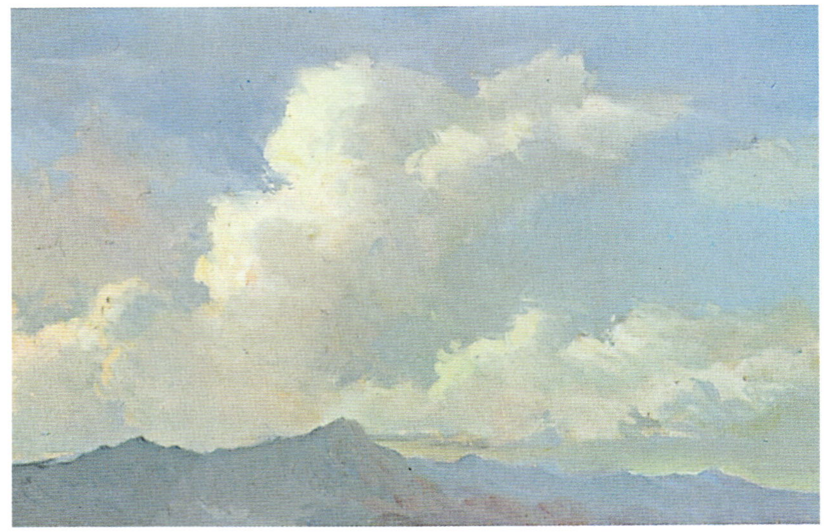

4. Cadmium Yellow Pale, Cadmium Red, Ultramarine Blue, Raw Umber.

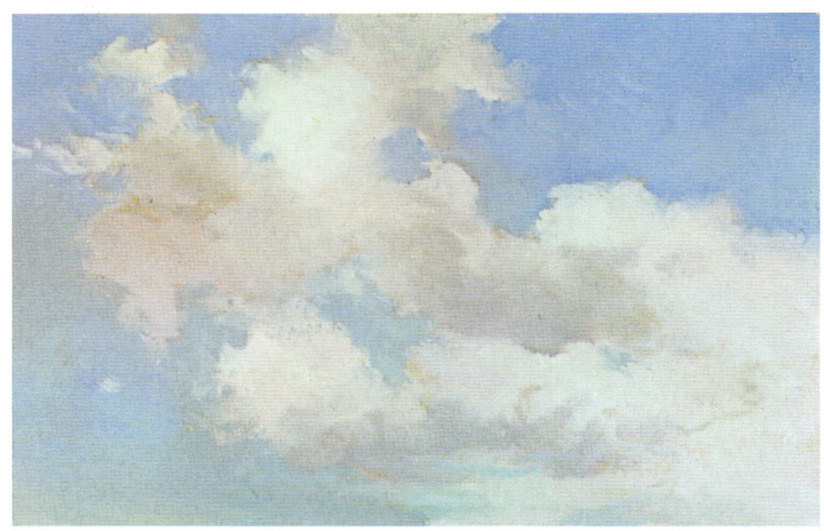

5. Cadmium Yellow Pale, Cadmium Red, Cobalt Blue, Paynes Gray.

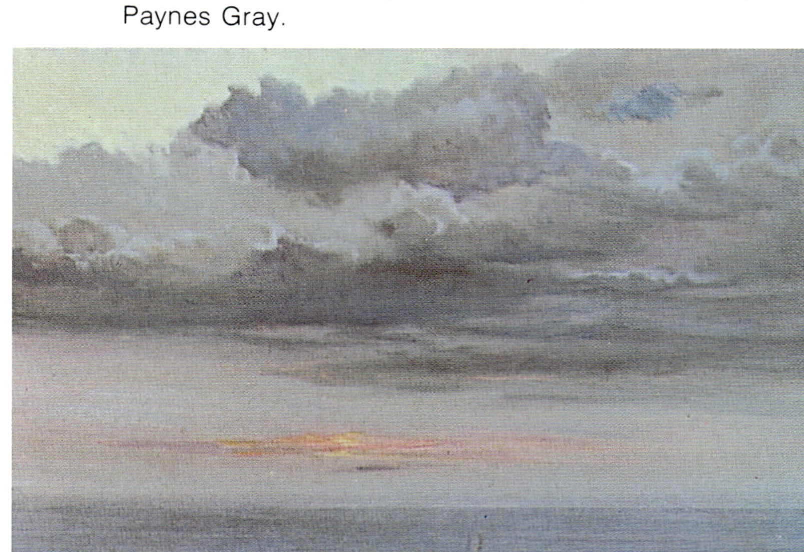

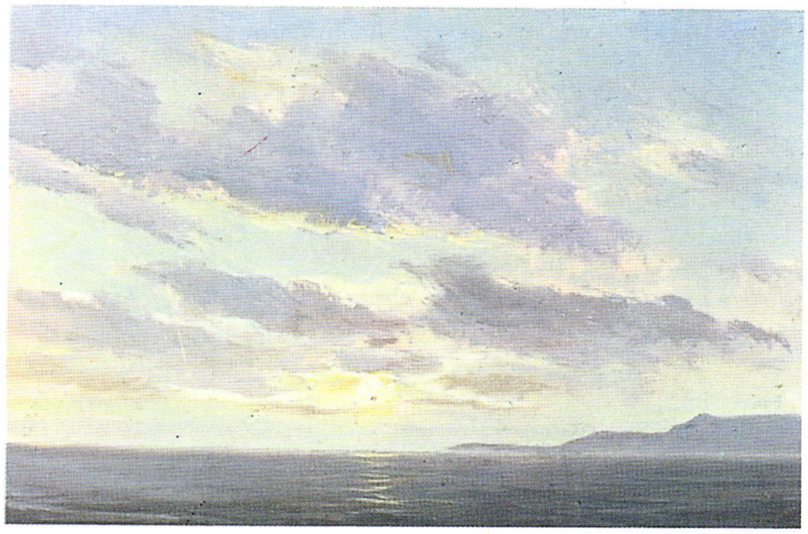

6. Cadmium Yellow Pale, Alizarin Crimson, Viridian Green, Paynes Grey.

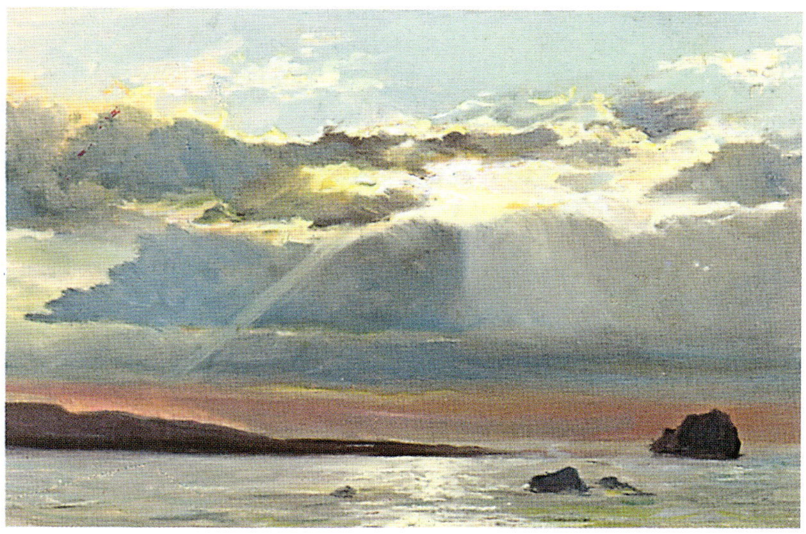

7. Cadmium Yellow Pale, Cadmium Red, Yellow Ochre, Cobalt Blue, Paynes Grey.

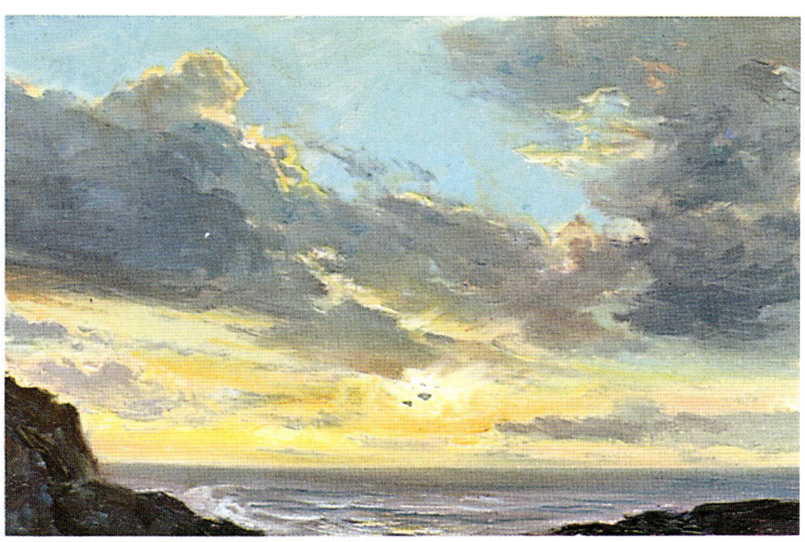

8. Cadmium Yellow Pale, Cadmium Yellow Deep, Cadmium Orange, Alizarin Crimson, Viridian Green, Cobalt Blue.

9. Cadmium Yellow Pale, Cadmium Orange, Alizarin Crimson, Raw Umber, Paynes Grey.

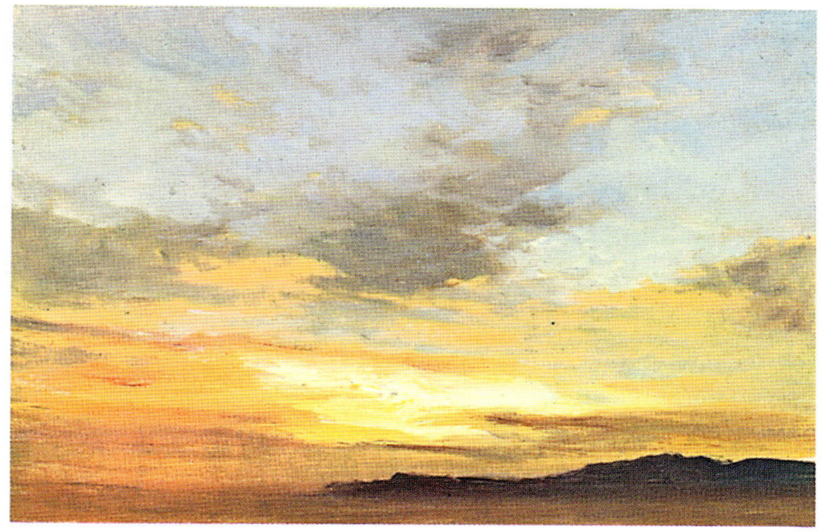

10. Cadmium Yellow Pale, Cadmium Orange, Cadmium Red, Alizarin Crimson, Cobalt Blue.

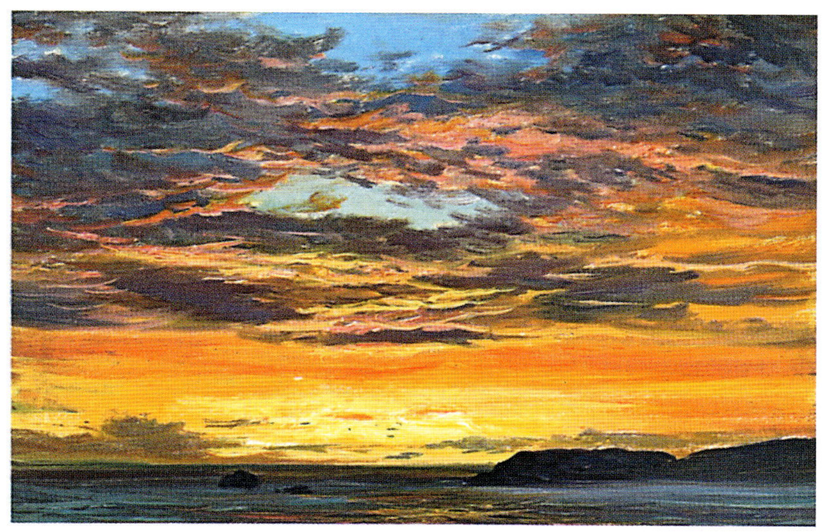

11. Cadmium Yellow Pale, Cadmium Orange, Cadmium Red, Alizarin Crimson, Viridian Green, Cobalt Blue.

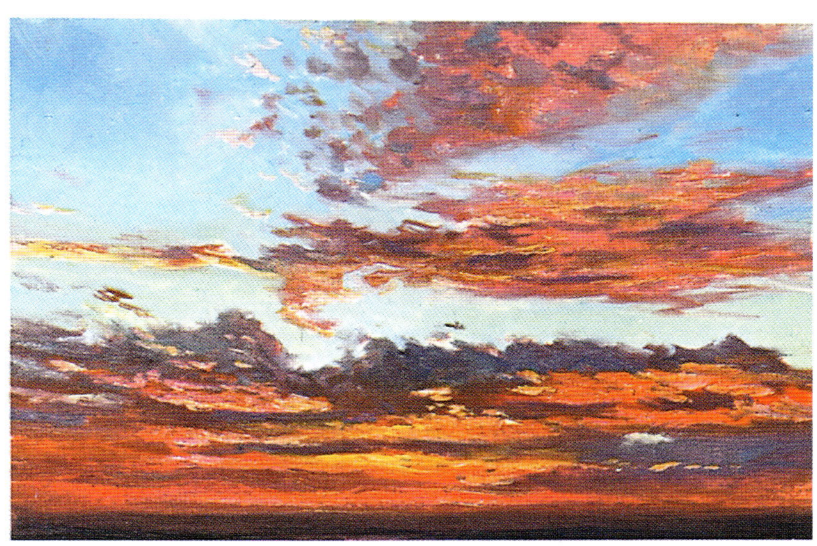

Cad. Yellow Pale
Alizarin Crimson
Viridian Green
Ultramarine Blue
Paynes Grey

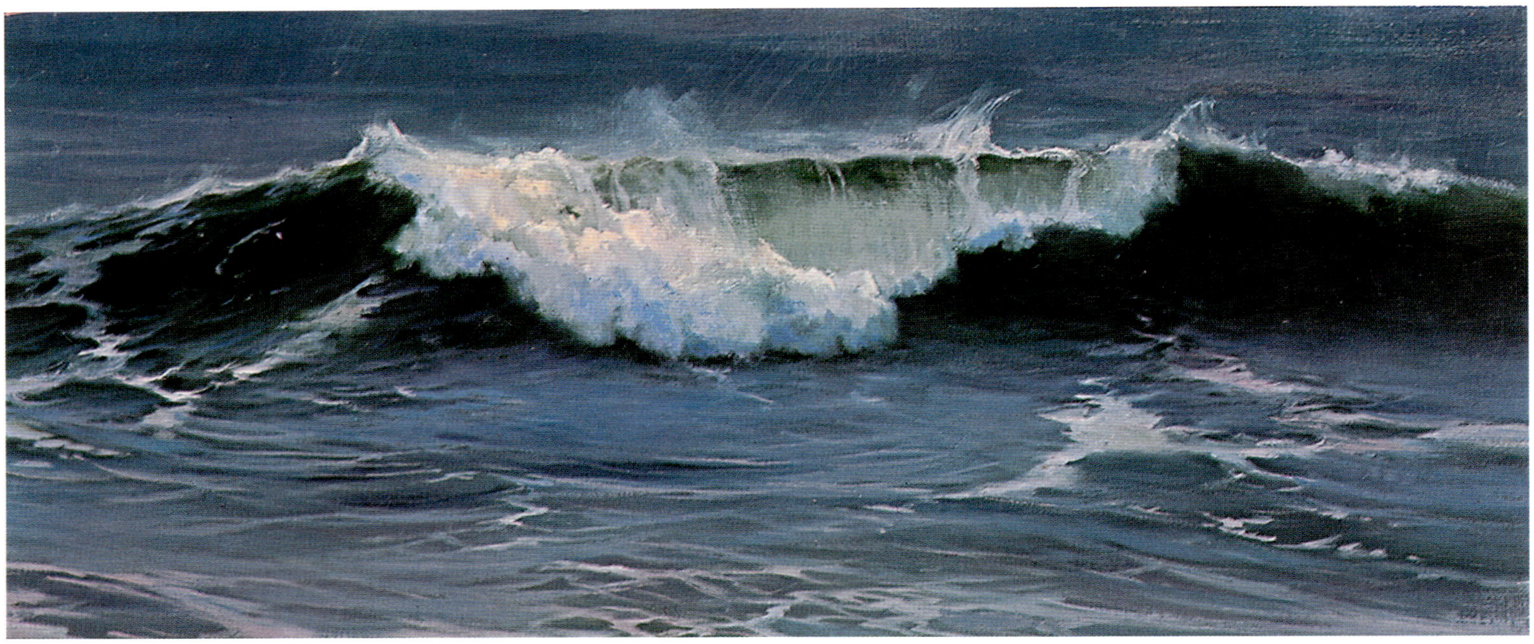

Cad. Yellow Pale
Yellow Ochre
Cad. Red Light
Alizarin Crimson
Cobalt Blue
Burnt Umber

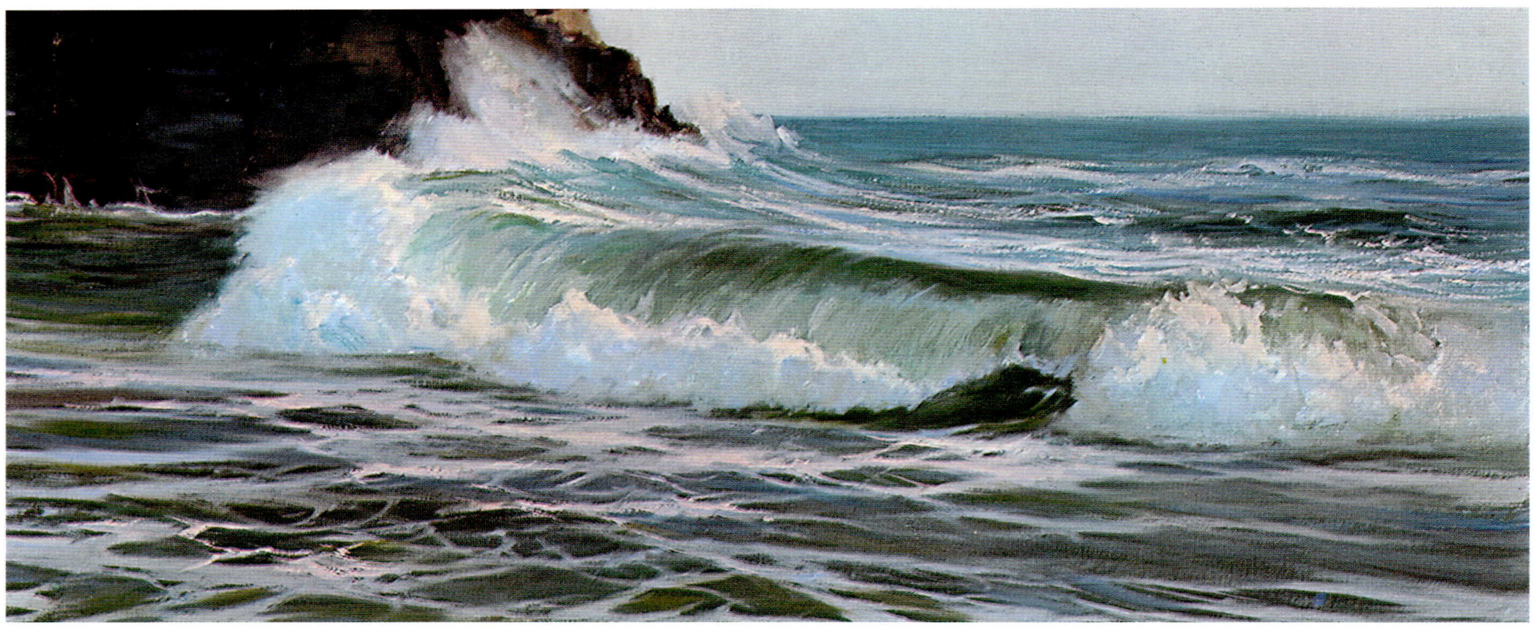

Cad. Yellow Pale
Yellow Ochre
Cad. Red Light
Viridian Green
Cerulean Blue
Cobalt Blue

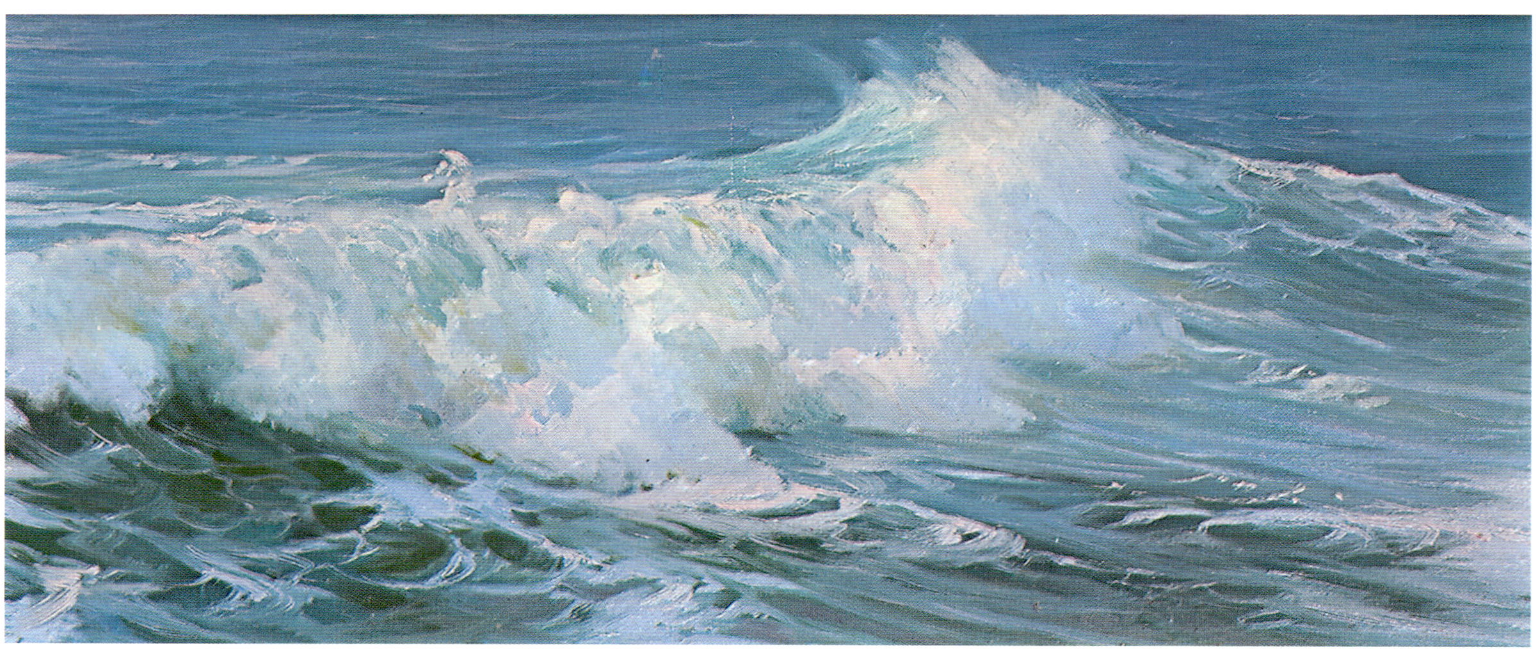

WAVE STUDIES. Variety is essential in becoming a good seascape artist. Study waves from different positions. Understand the force that creates a wave. Watch the wake patterns in the foam and form of the water after the wave passes. The curl of a wave is usually shaped like a tube, but it can often be met by an angular swell, as in the bottom picture. Notice that the force of the wave creates chunks of foam as it hits; to make these cnunks too soft-looking would weaken the strength of the wave. Never use pure white in painting foam, as that makes it look like cotton. Rely instead on the premixed shades of paint to achieve tonal contract (warm against cool).

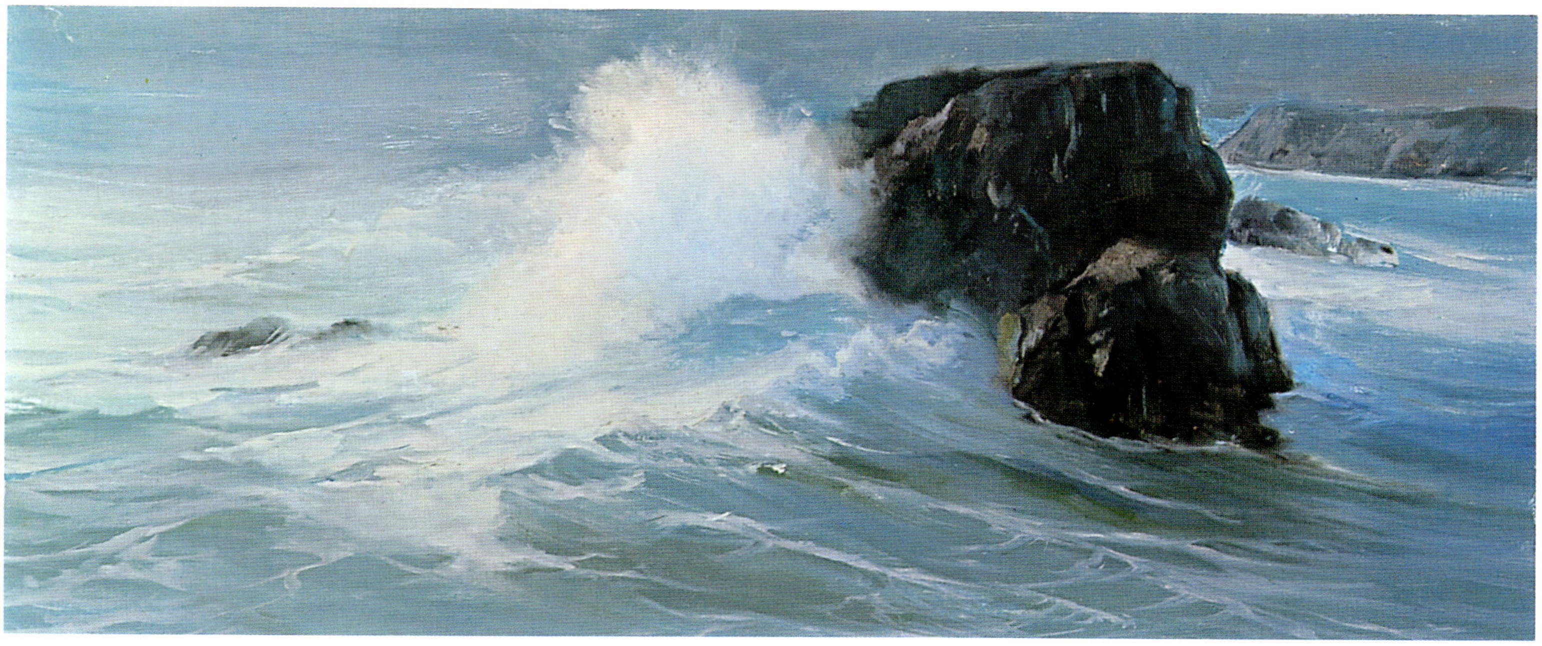

Cad. Yellow Pale
Alizarin Crimson
Viridian Green
Ultramarine Blue
Paynes Gray

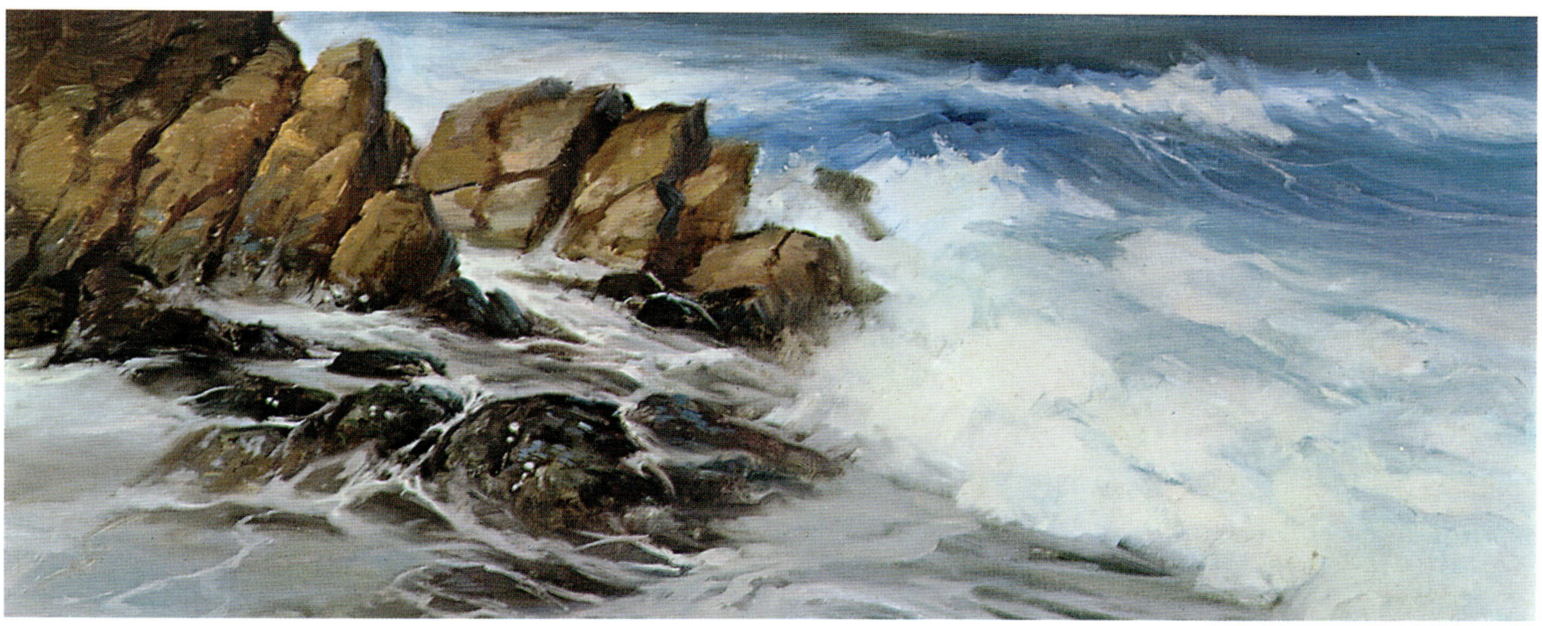

Cad. Yellow Pale
Yellow Ochre
Cad. Red Light
Alizarin Crimson
Cobalt Blue
Burnt Umber

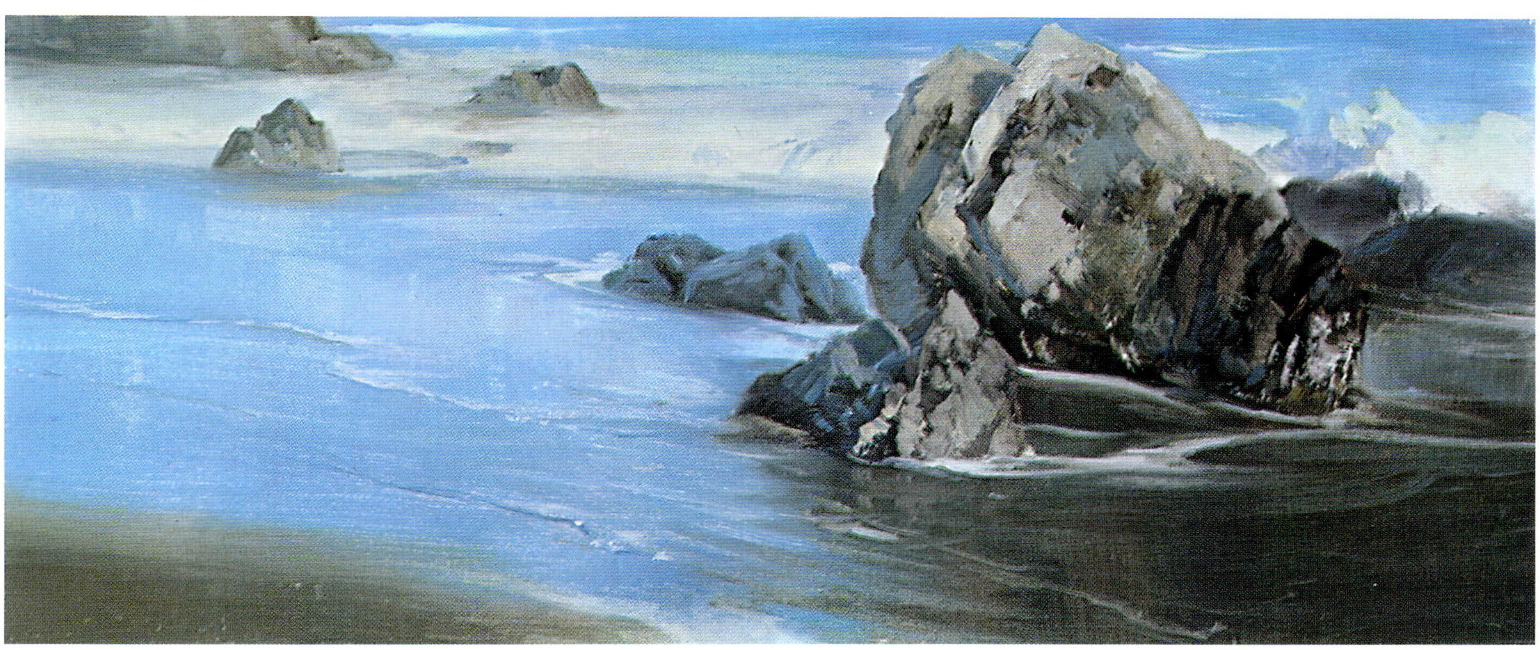

Cad. Yellow Pale
Yellow Ochre
Cad. Red Light
Viridian Green
Cerulean Blue
Cobalt Blue

ROCK STUDIES. There is about as much difference in rock shapes and colors as there is in wave formations. Understand the kind of rock you are trying to portray. Is it rounded, stratified, blocky, or pitted like lava? Is it reddish, brown, gray, black, blue? Is it wet? Strong paintings need angular rocks to portray their strength. To harmonize a rock with its surroundings, vary the color by intensity and grays, and bring some of the background color into the rock. In still water, carry the rock color into the reflections to make the rock "sit down." Sometimes I change a rock shape in my painting to create a better design, but I try not to lose the character of the rock itself.

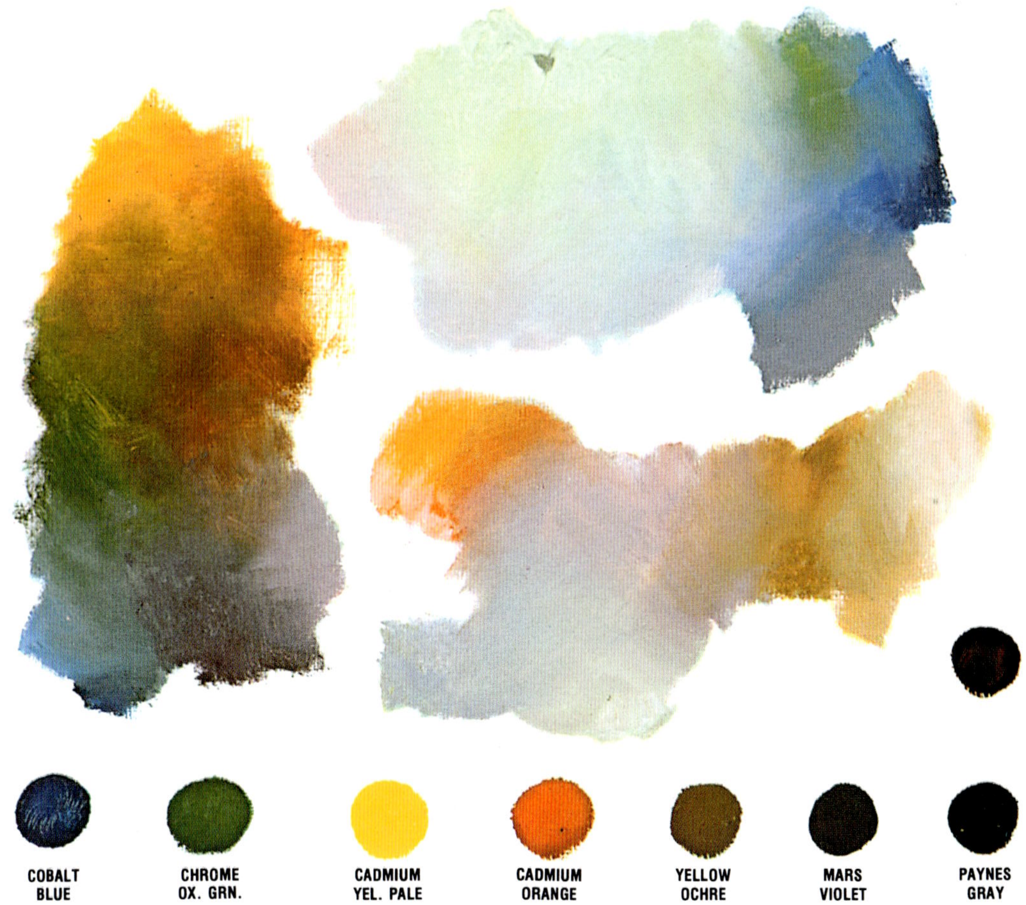

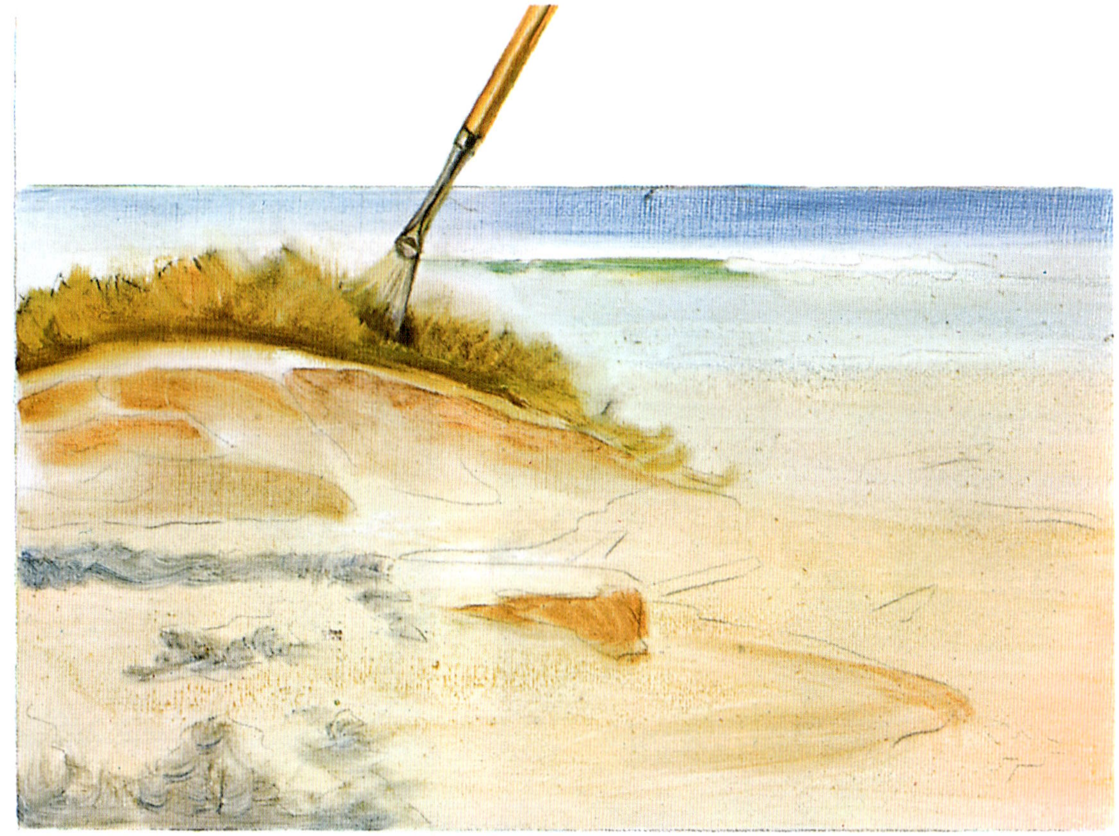

Keep the colors under the grasses rich and clean. Use a fan blender to create up-swept strokes.

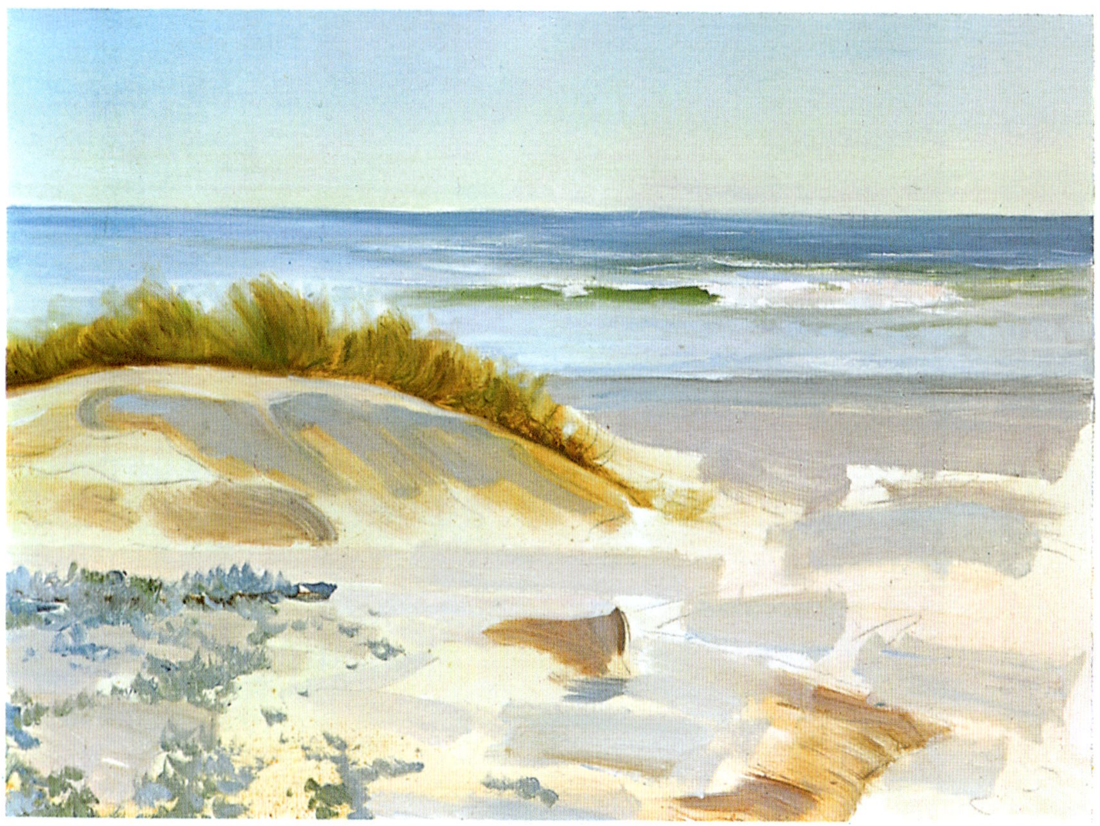

Here the key colors are Mars Violet and Cadmium Orange. The shadow areas inside the dunes are the critical areas in this painting.

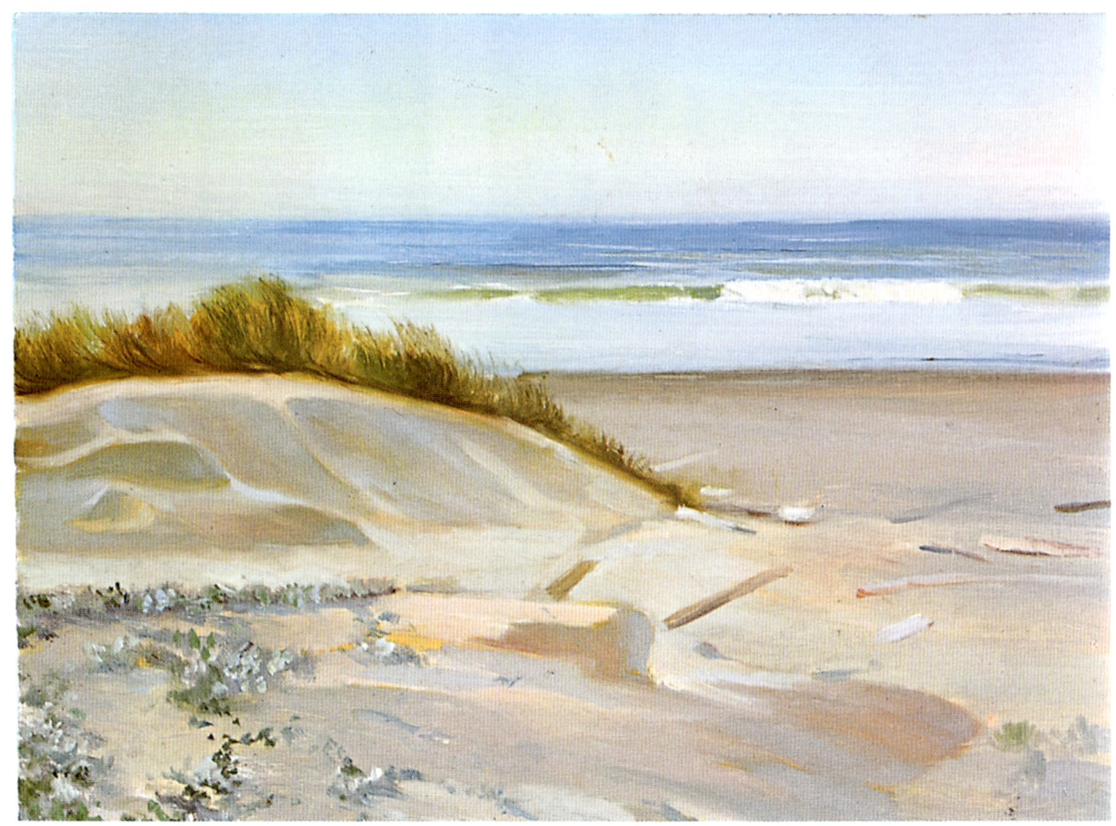

The intense warm colors inside the shadow areas will create life in a seemingly colorless picture. This applies to desert painting as well.

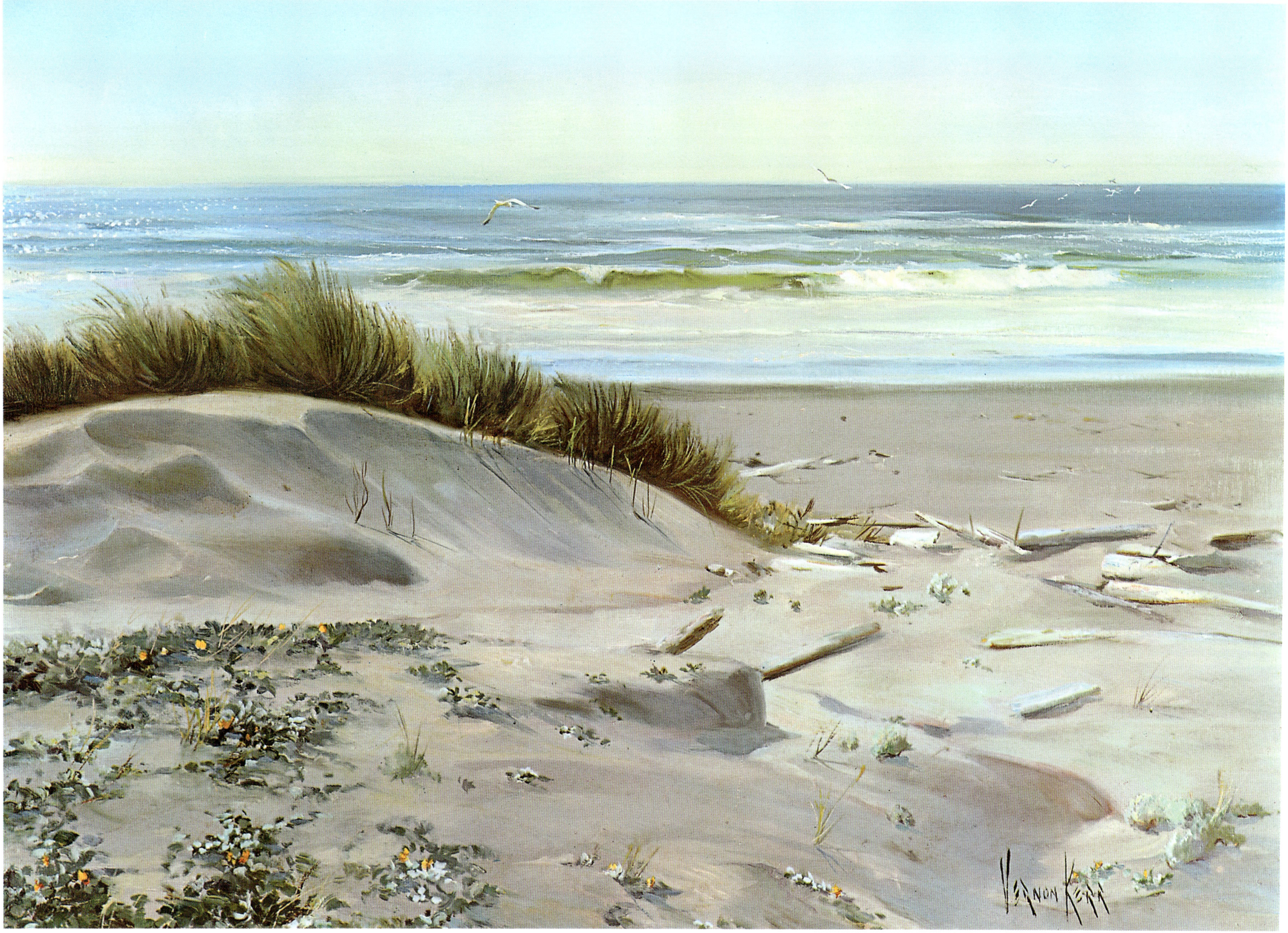

SEA DUNES. Values on a sunlit day are deceiving. A warm color seems to be lighter than a cool color of the same value. When two values of different colors appear to be the same, merge them together to make them less poster-like. Hold a long bristle brush parallel to the canvas and softly merge the colors. Use a large brush; a small one would create the look of fussiness.

The mood of tranquility created in the foreground of this painting was more important to me than a breaking wave. The grasses are swaying in the wind. The driftwood is half-buried in the sand (notice the soft edges). The plants send runners in a rhythmic pattern across the dunes. Seagulls drift in the breeze. Smell the salt air? Feel the sun on your back? Now you're getting it!

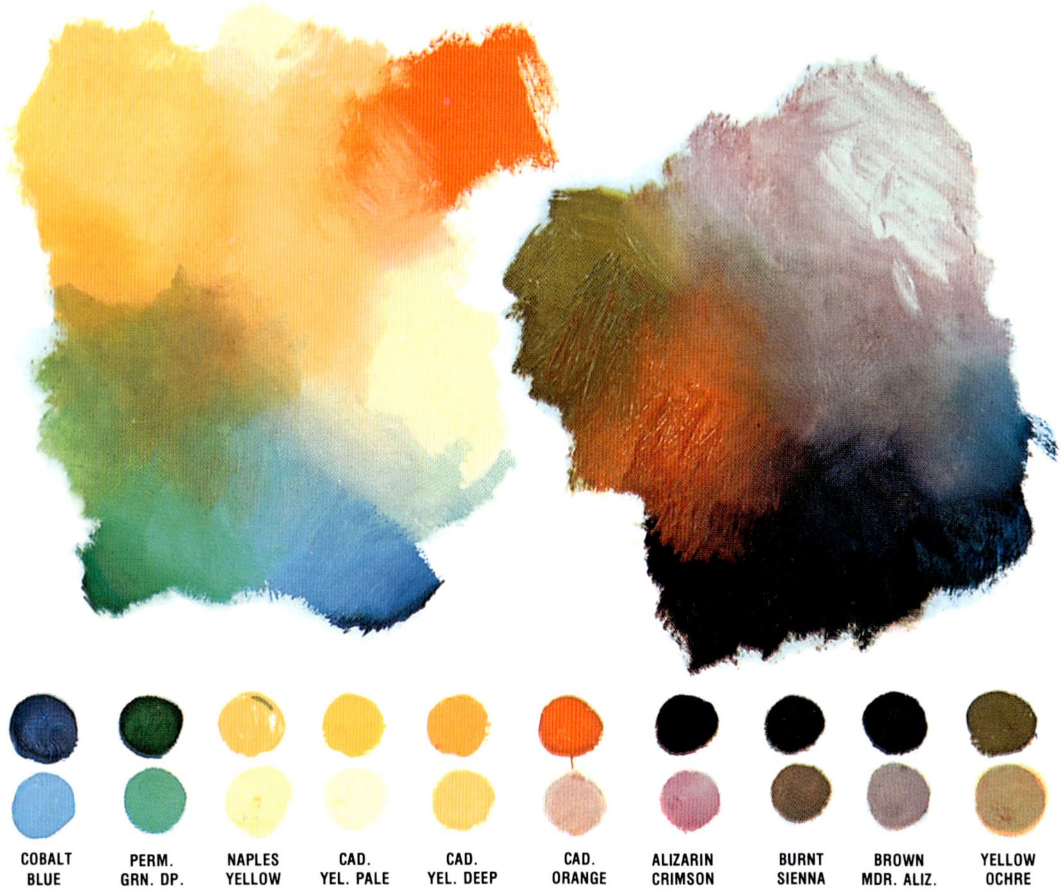

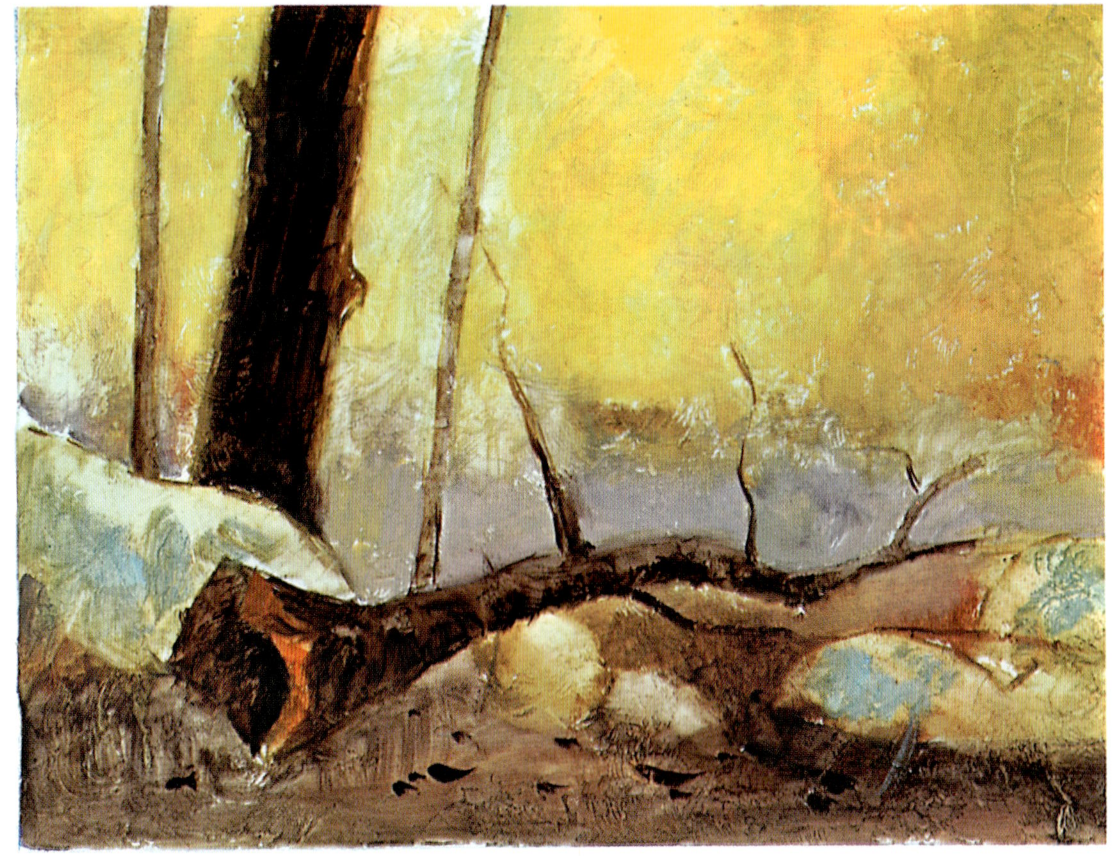

Turp wash with Naples Yellow. Try to keep the background clean. Establish darks with Brown Madder Alizarin on the tree trunk.

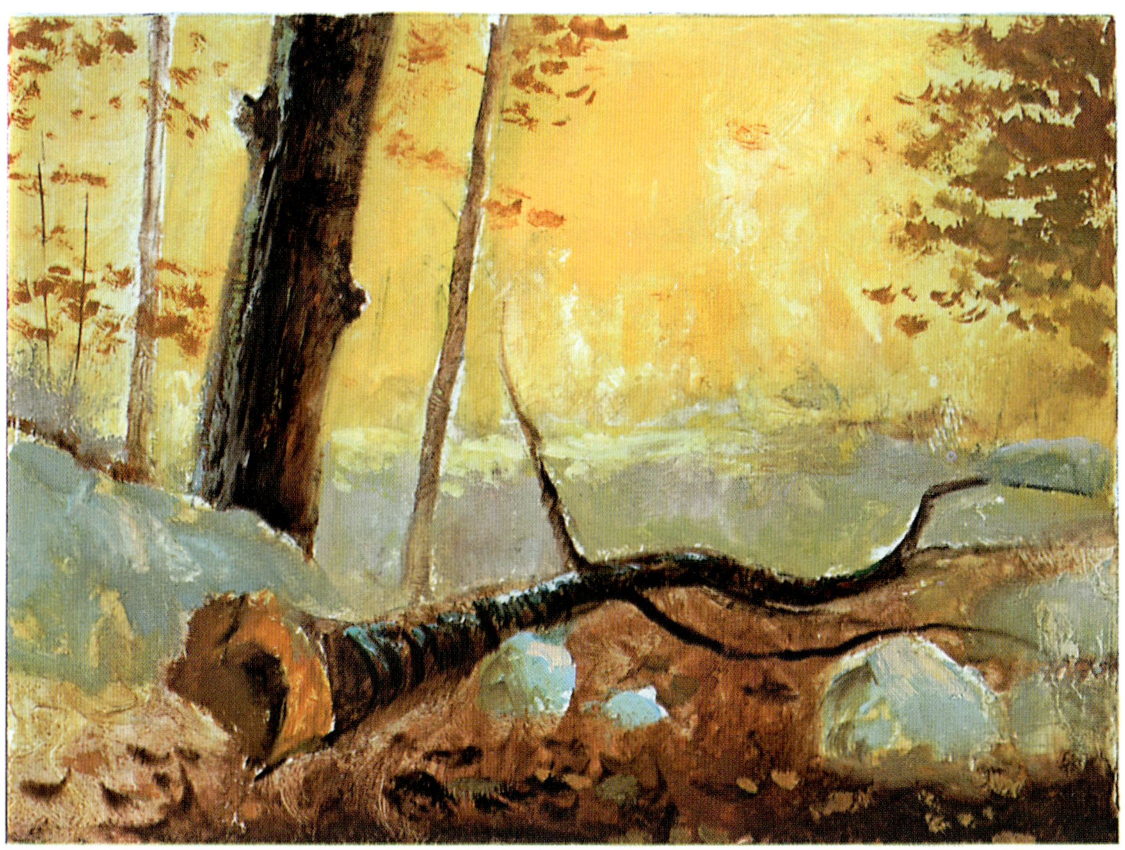

Painting ACROSS THE FORM of the fallen limb has many advantages: It makes the limb solid and gives it perspective and foreshortening.

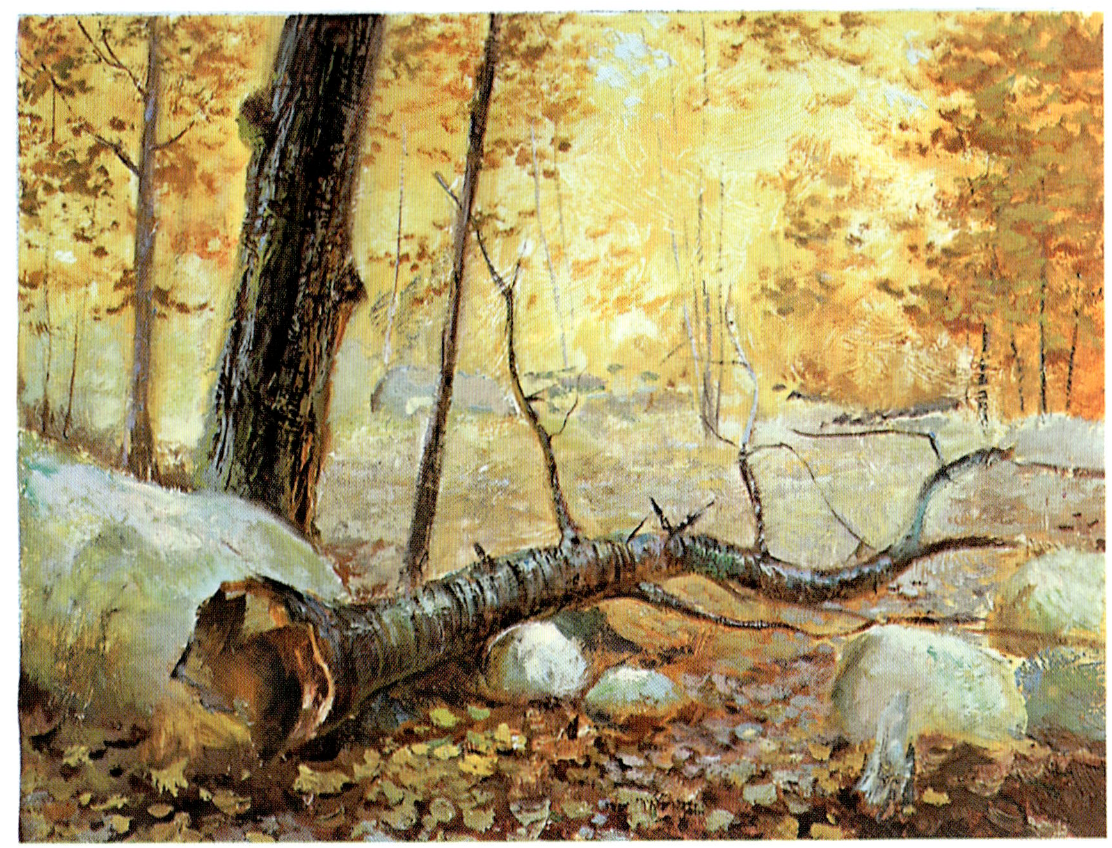

It also adds more texture to the bark. To achieve roundness (or a wrap-around quality), make the edges soft and add reflected lights.

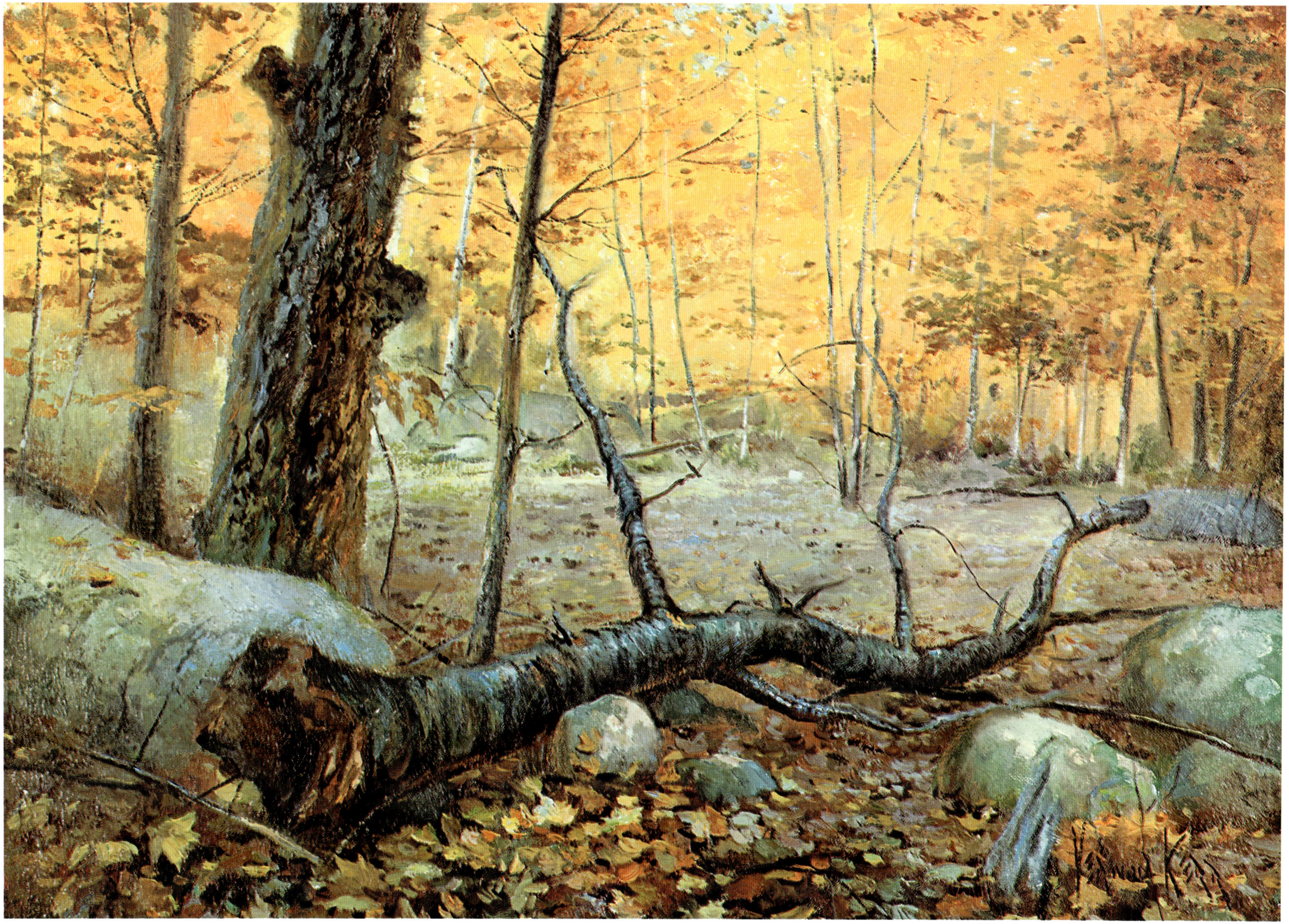

AUTUMN LULLABY. Fallen leaves are especially intriguing, but sometimes hard to paint. The idea is to make them appear to be many, without painting each one. I used a textured canvas. First wash in an earth color of Brown Madder Alizarin and Burnt Sienna. Build up the leaf texture using a round bristle brush.

Remember that the leaves are decaying, so be sure to vary the colors and include mauve tones and grays. The fresh leaves on top have richer colors. In the foreground, make the strokes crisper and blur the leaves that are far away. Do not overblend or you will get dead color. Accent a few darks to make the leaves "lay down."

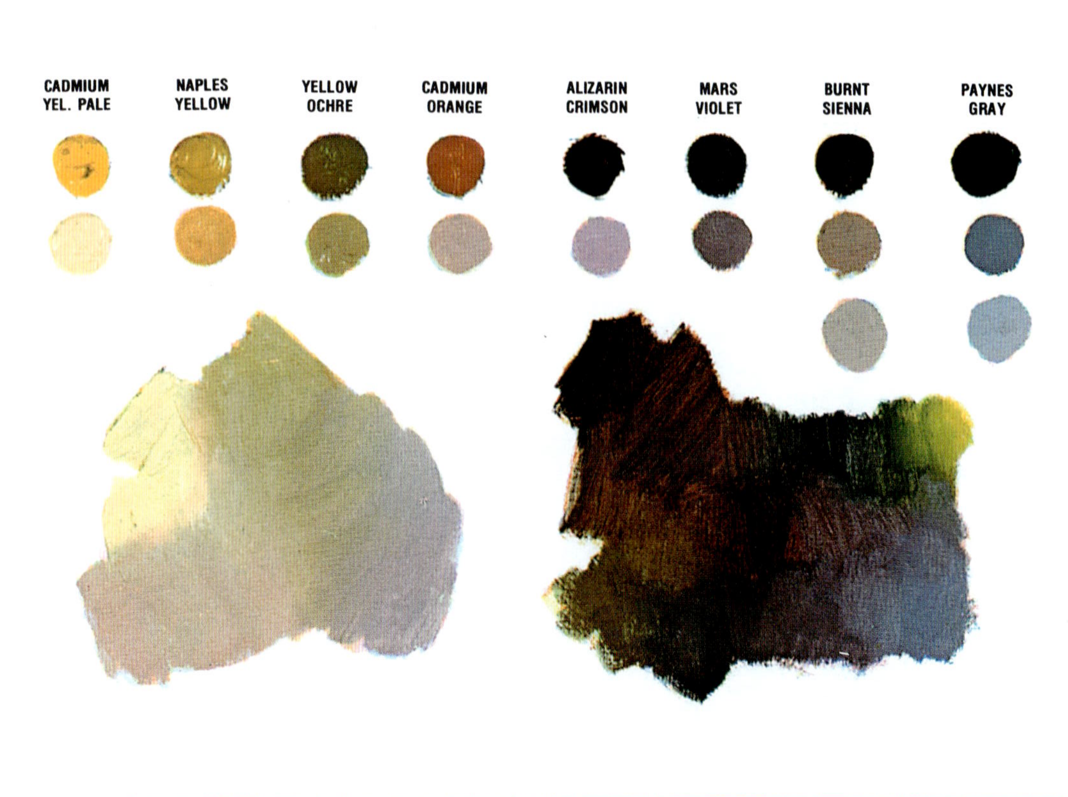

Mix large palette spectrums first. The spectrum on the left carries sky and water colors, and the right one is rocks and sand.

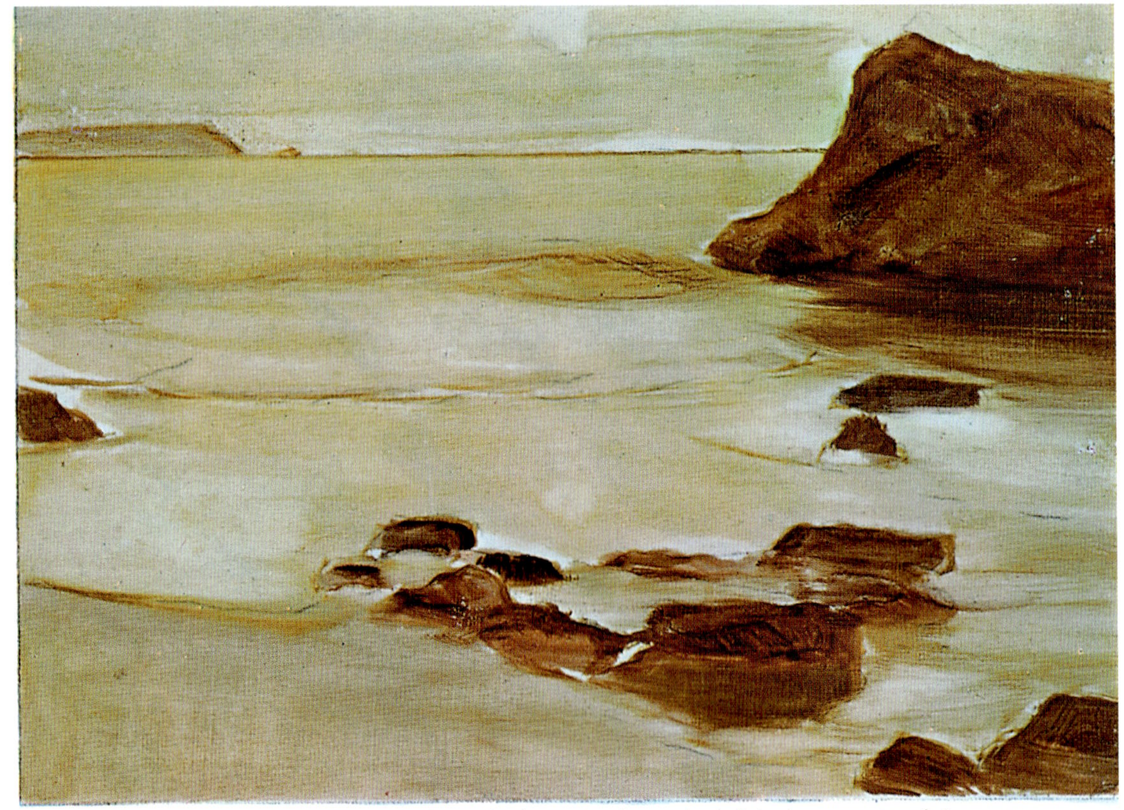

Glaze the undertone with the glazing medium. Let this tone carry into your final painting, especially in the rocks.

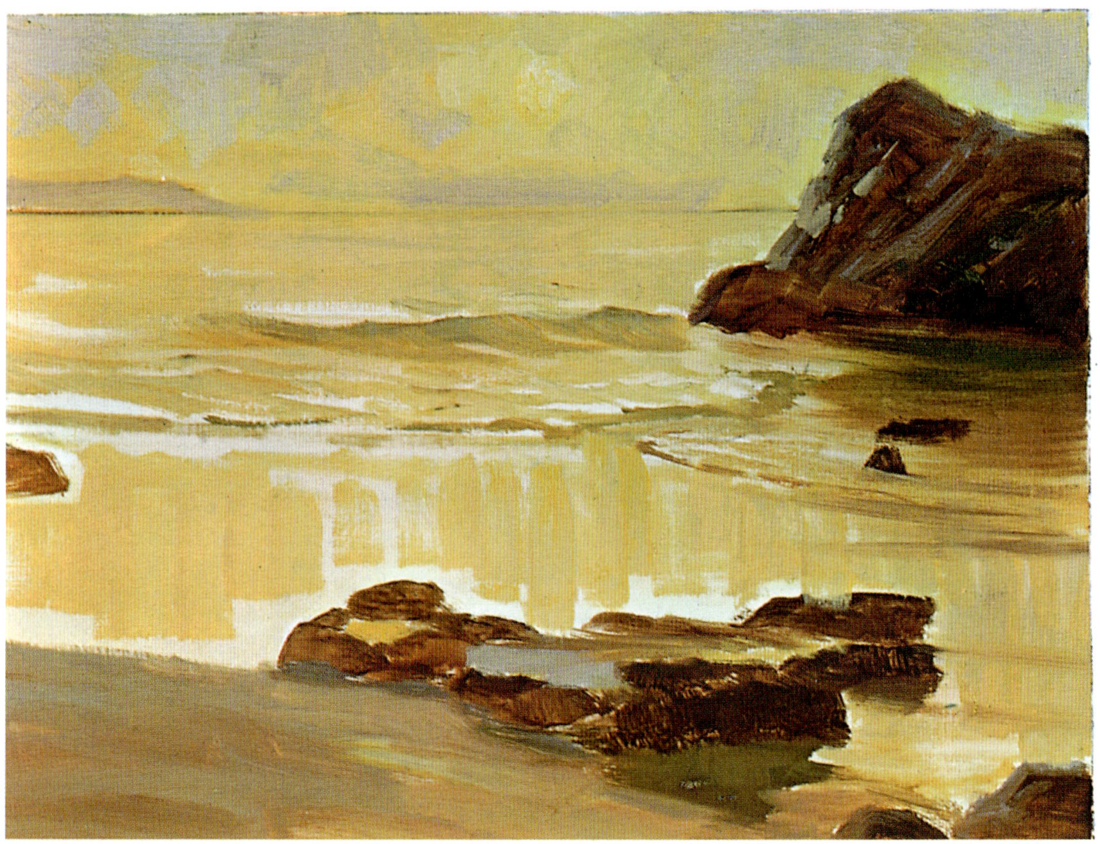

Reflections are achieved with vertical strokes of color where the beach is wet. Try not to blend. Do not lose the vertical strokes.

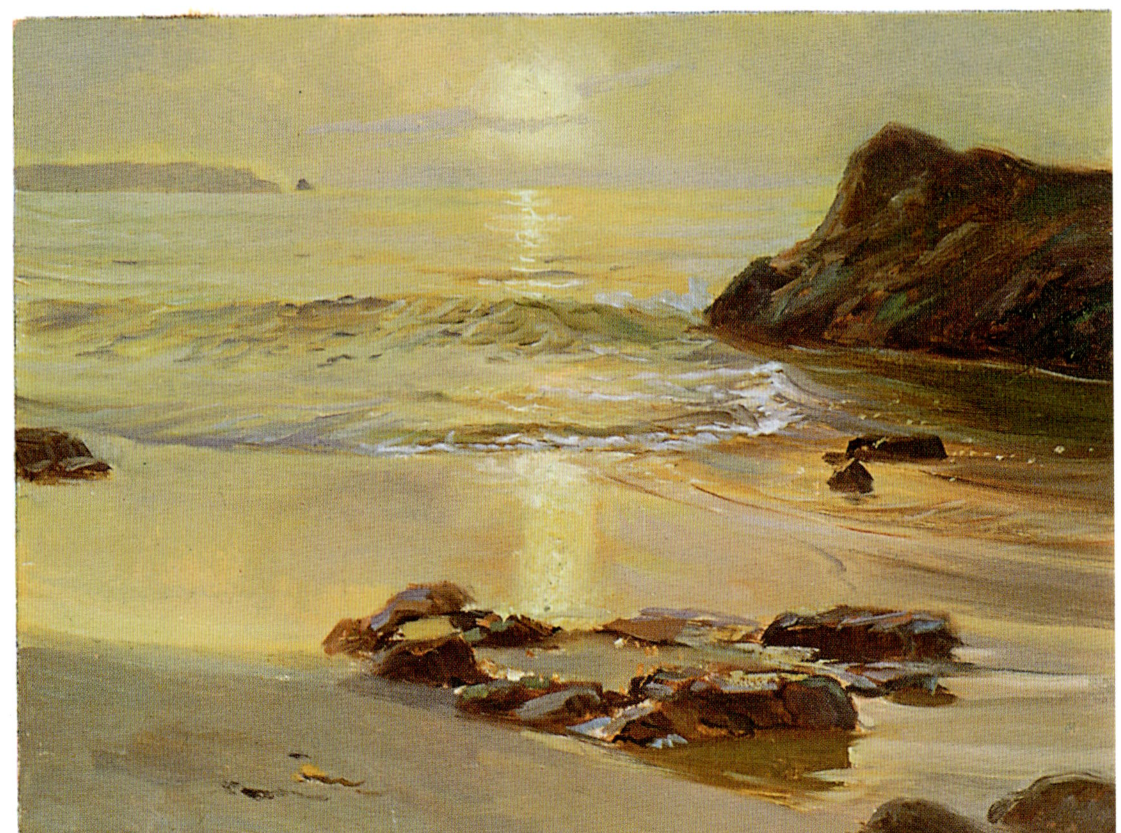

To portray water movement on a shiny beach, cut across the vertical strokes slightly with a large soft blender. Add details when dry.

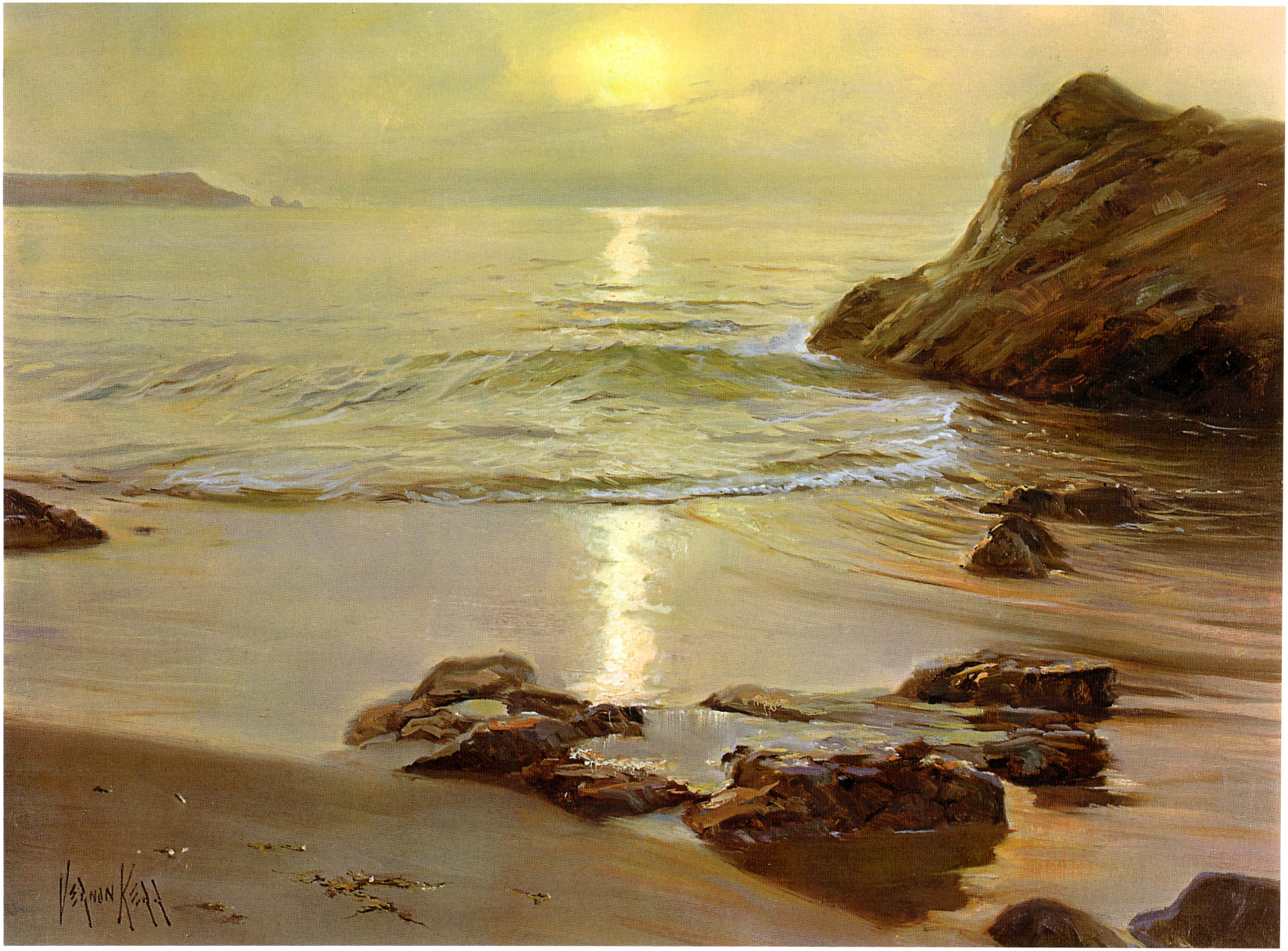

AWAKENING SUNSET. From my dining-room window I can watch the brilliant sunsets over the Pacific. I'm fascinated by the multitude of color schemes that the casual visitor might never see. Notice how I've carried the same colors from the sky through the sand. The lavenders and yellows balance each other.

To give the sun's reflection, build up thick dimensional paint in the areas where the sunshine would seem to hit. Let the thick strokes dry, and scumble over them with a lighter value, but not white. Thereafter, light cast upon the painting will refract from the surface of the strokes and add to the sunshiny effect.

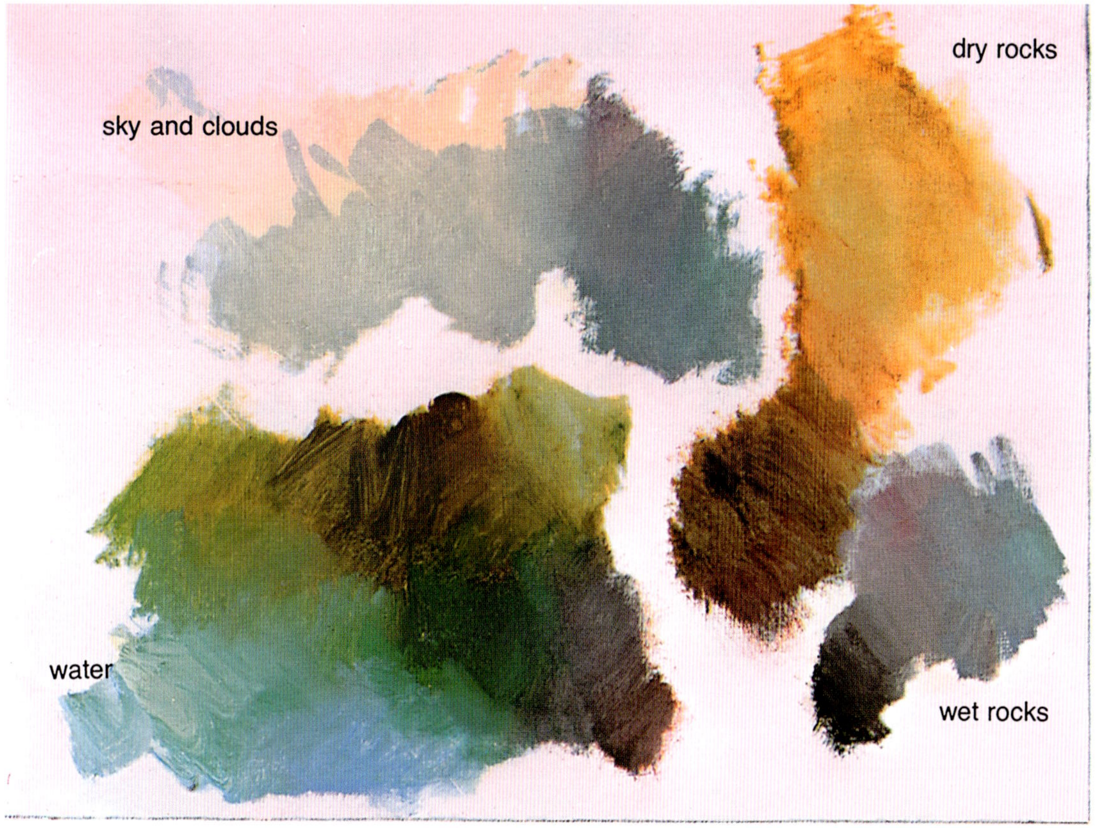

Cad. Yellow Pale, Cad. Orange, Alizarin Crimson, Phthalo Yellow-Green, Viridian Green, Cobalt Blue, Yellow Ochre, Burnt Sienna, Raw Umber.

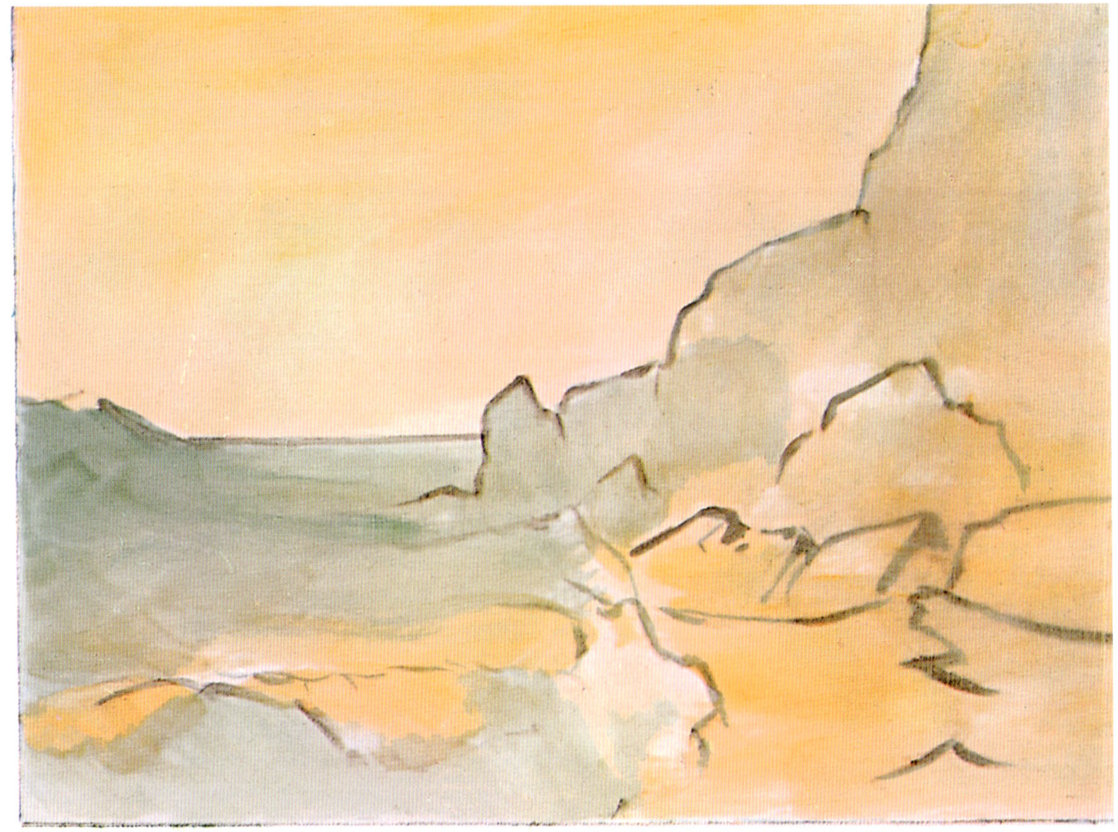

It is not important to match my colors exactly, so long as your colors harmonize with each other and create a good tone.

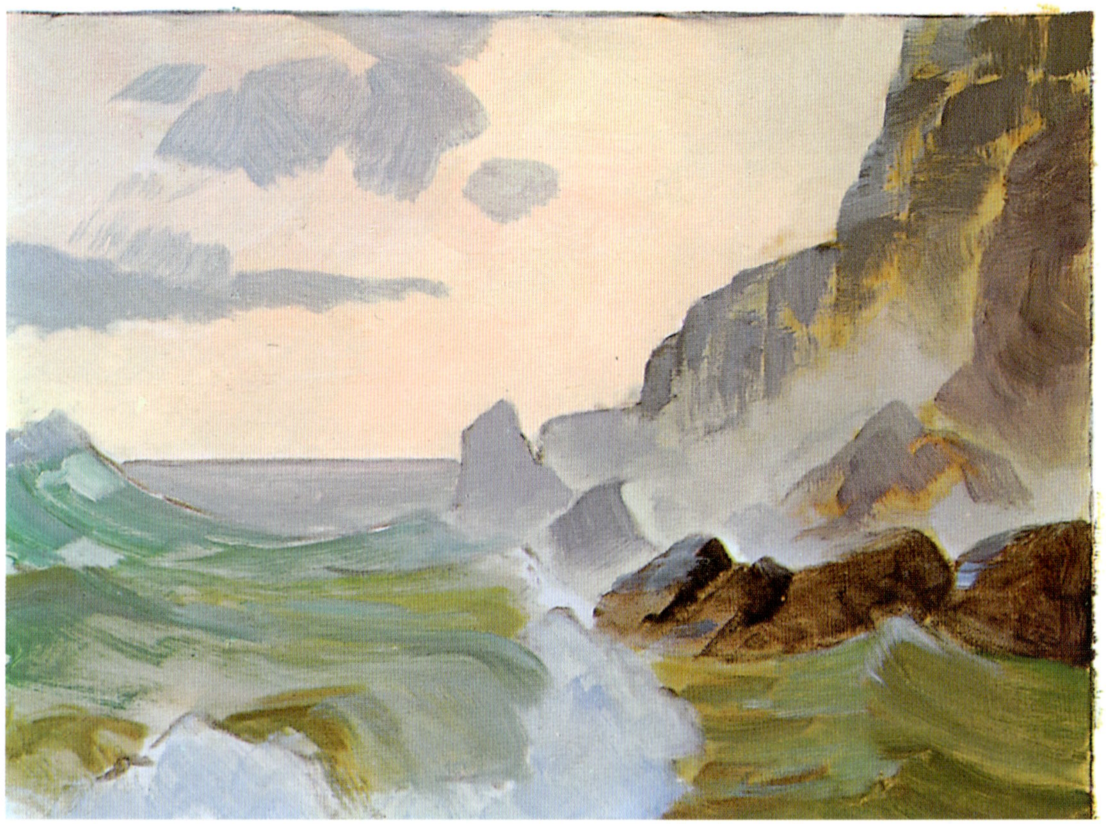

Contrast of WARM against COOL gives the illusion of more values. Control values by relying on premixes and the palette spectrum.

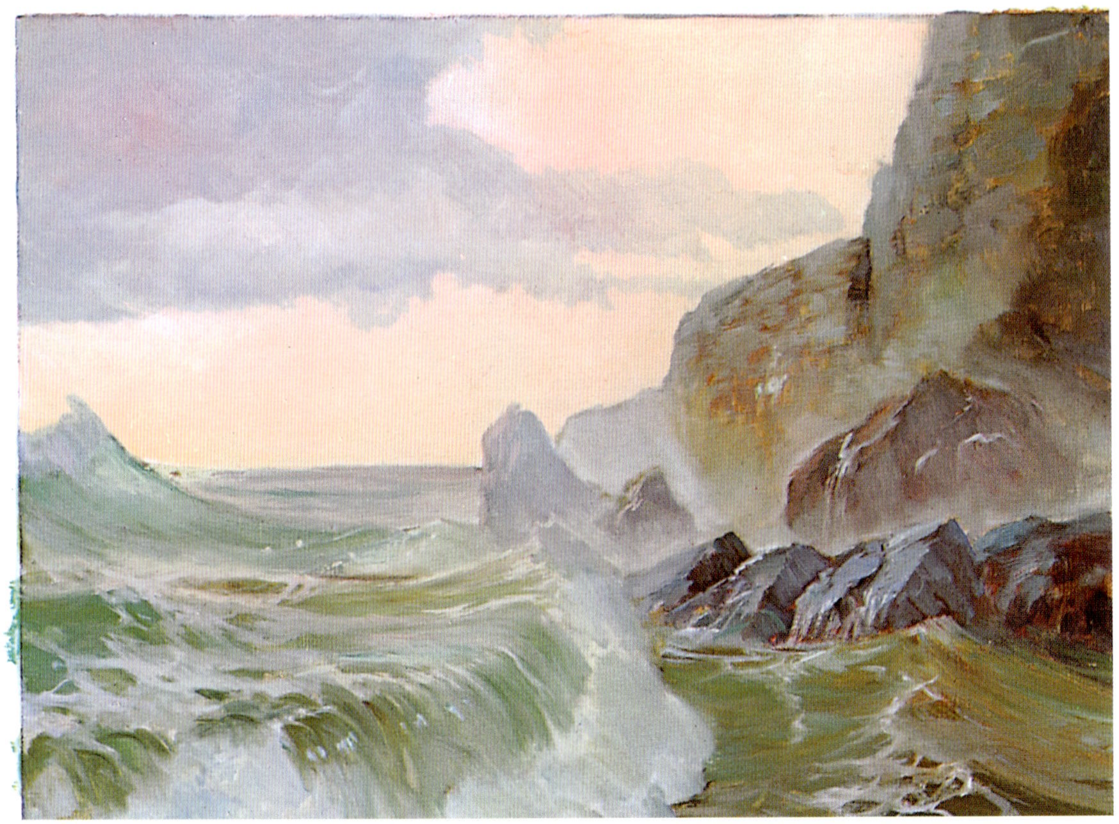

Mix lots of grays. This does not mean using blacks-and-whites! If a color is too intense, blend it with a complementary color.

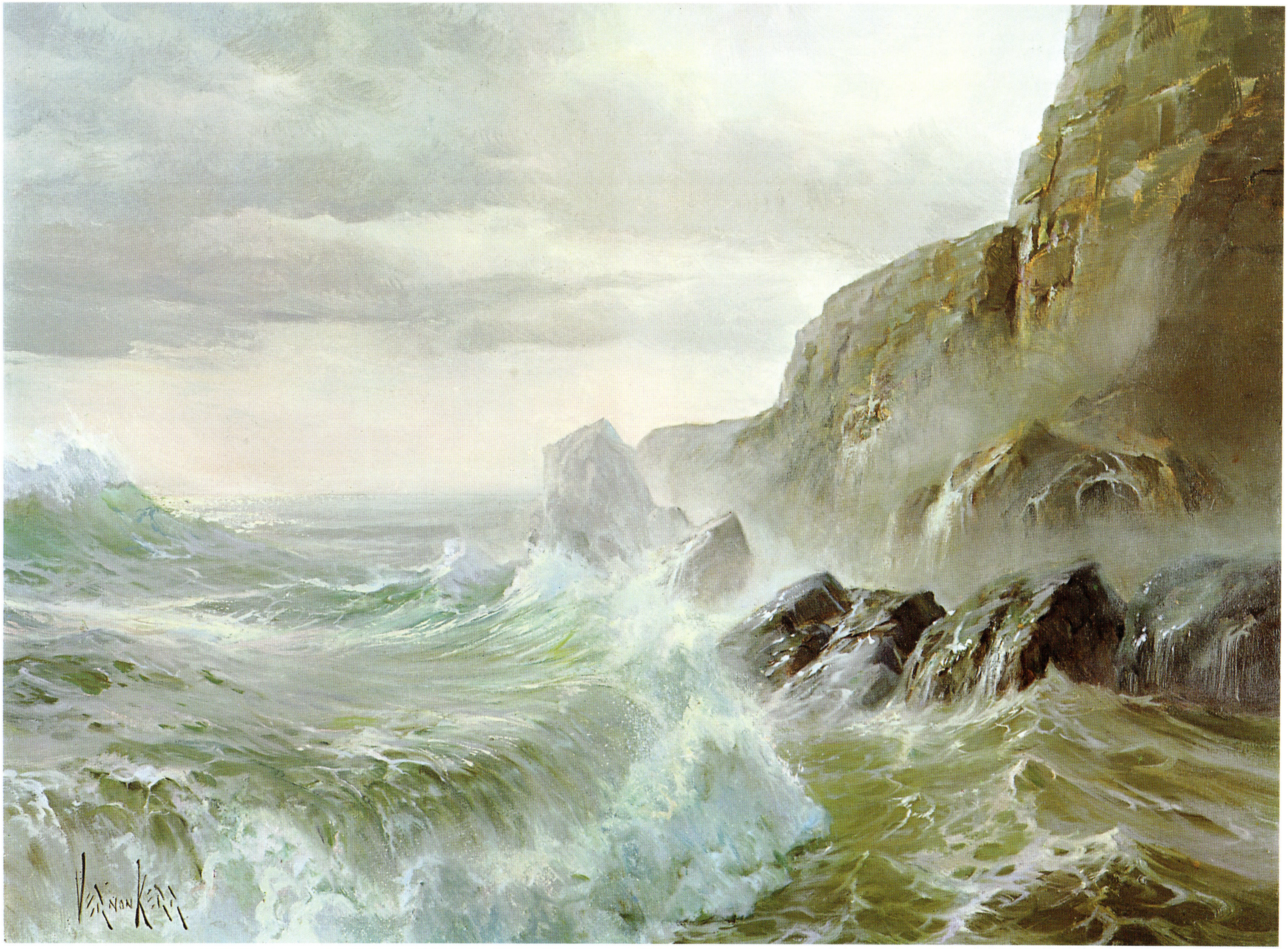

THE CITADELS. Fog to me is mystical and mysterious. The colors are subtle and beautiful. The mistake often made in painting fog is to make it too washed out. The overall value for this picture is #5, with all other values between #4 and #6, except for the dark rocks.

One can see the actual color of the water itself when the sun is hidden. There are no strong colors or values in this painting. If yours become too intense, tone the intensity when the painting is dry by glazing a complementary color on the surface. Wipe off the excess until the desired tone is accomplished.

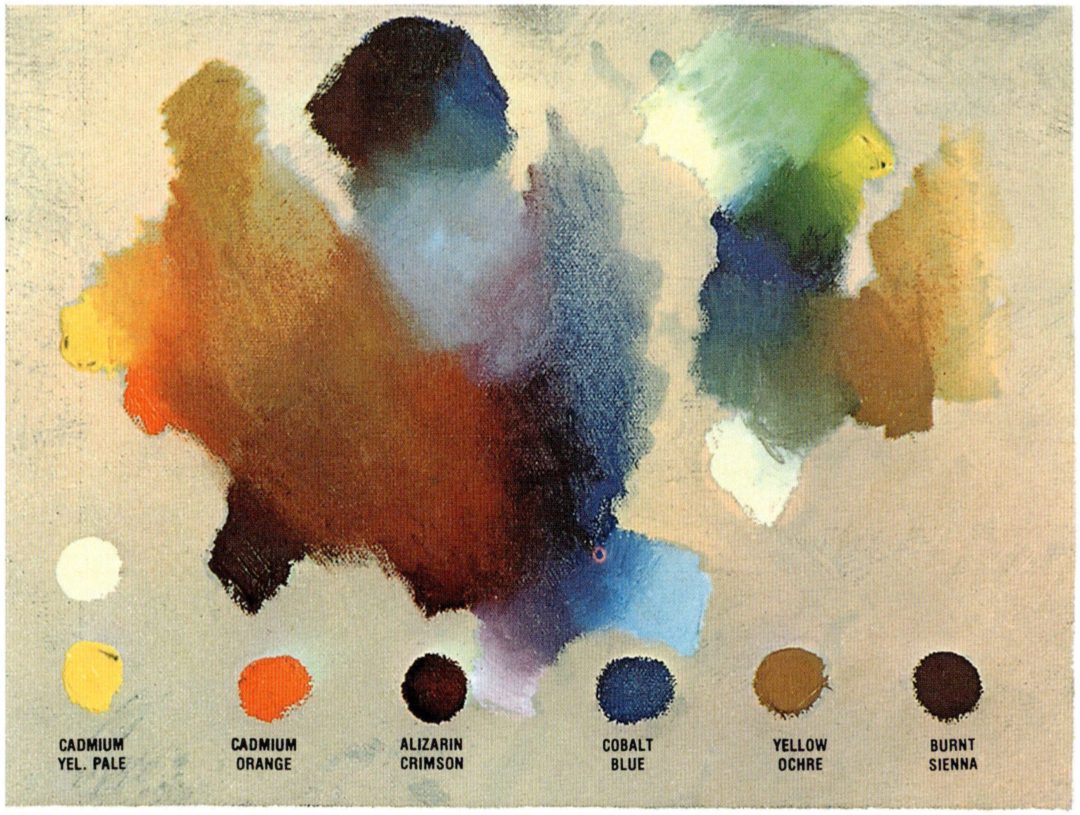

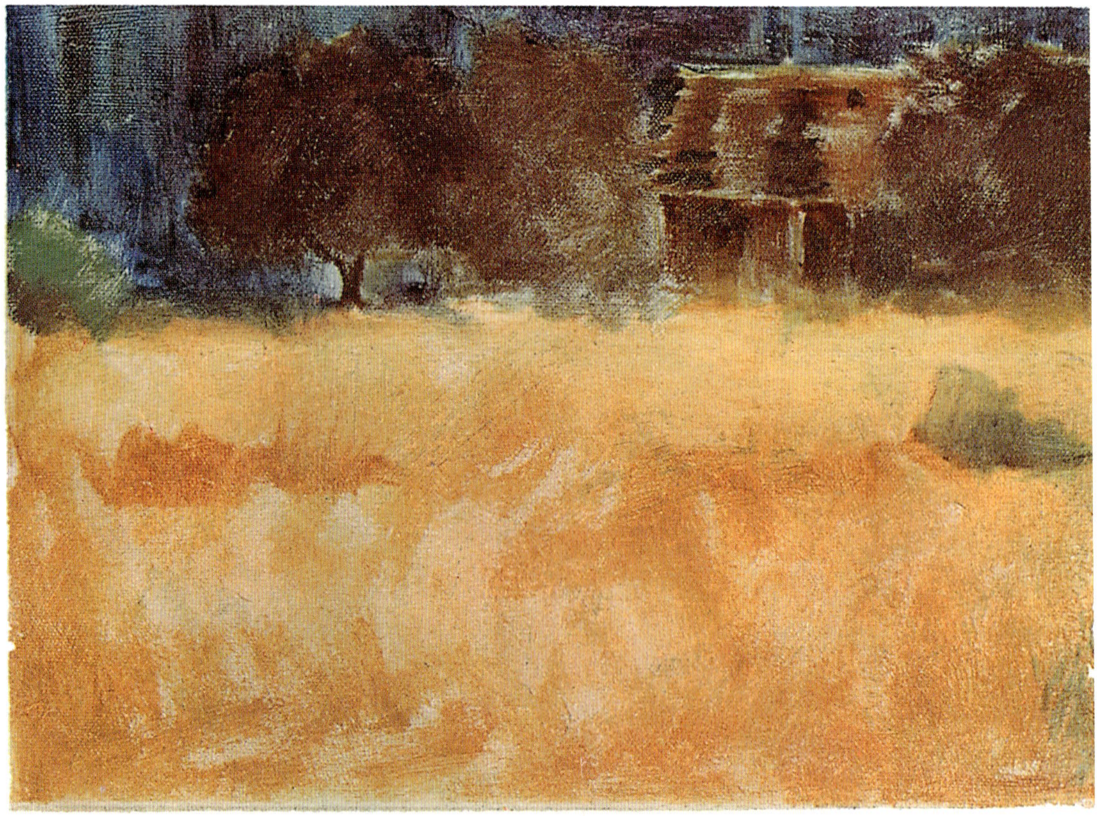

Tone with varnish-turp-oil mixture. Be accurate in tone. If underpainting is too light or too dark, the overpainting won't look right.

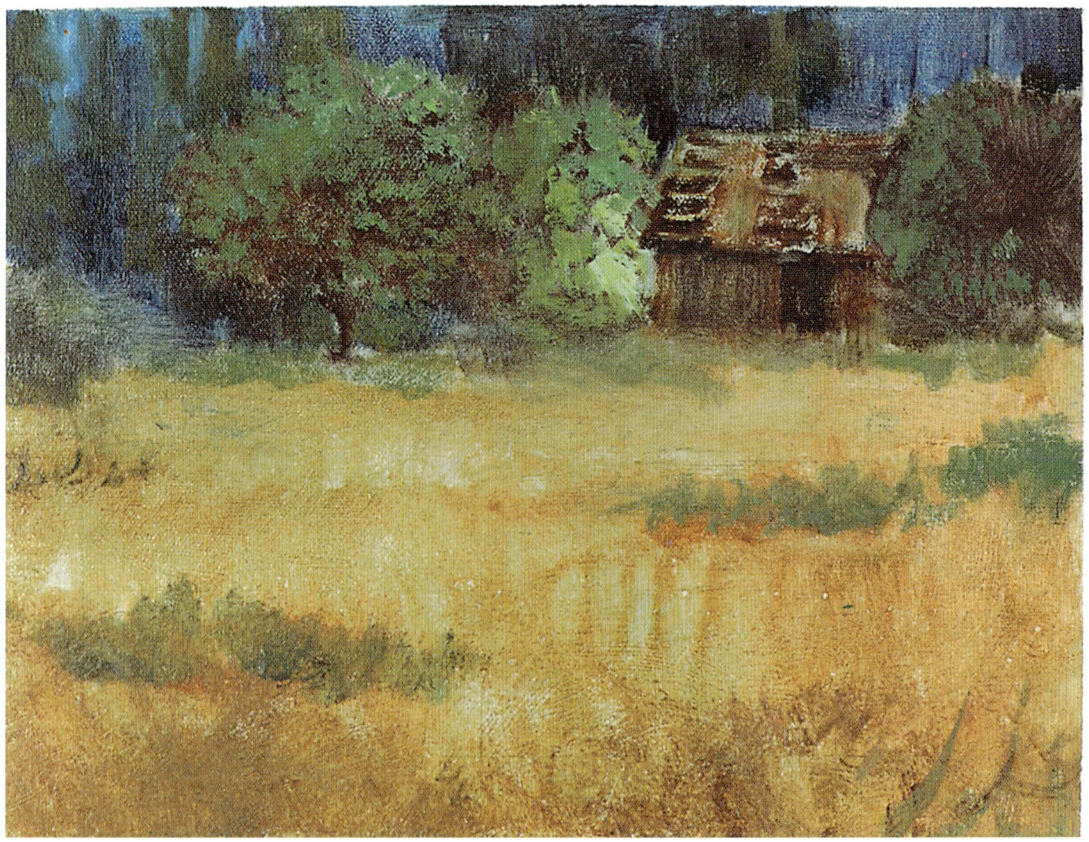

The grass in this painting is simple color pattern with few details. The daisies are patches of tone in distance, with details up close.

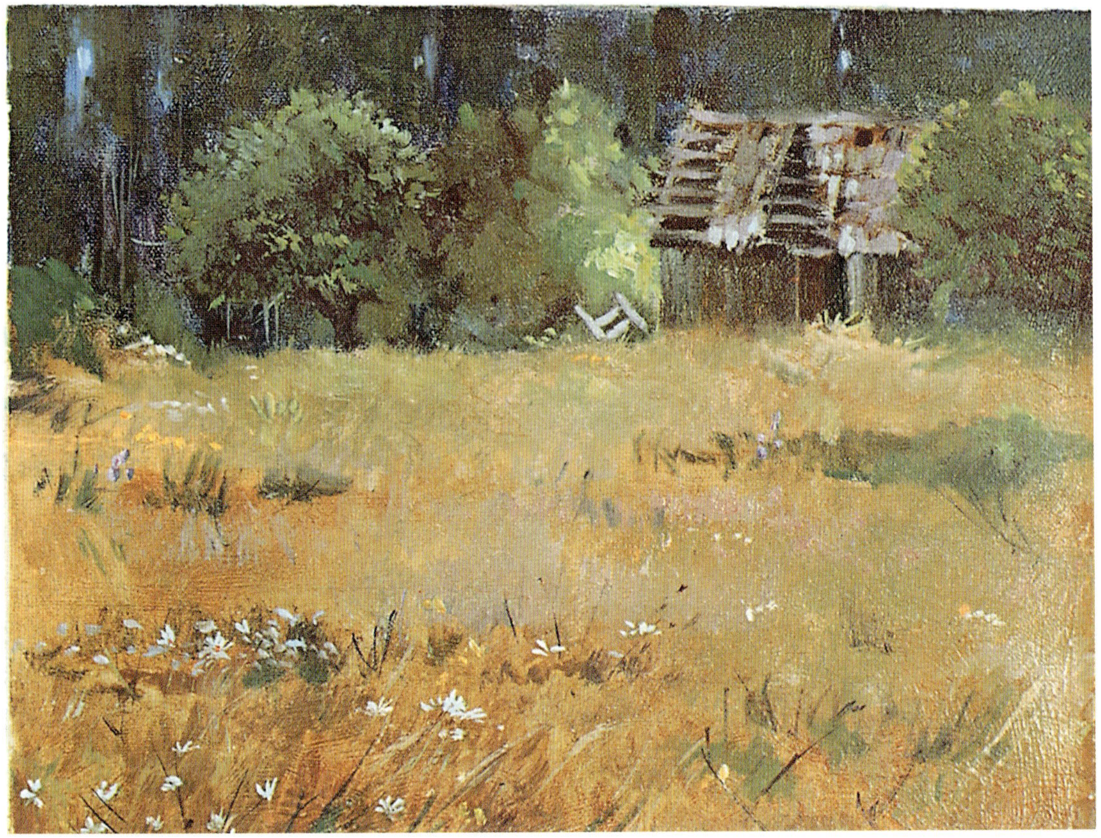

The lavender shades, complementary to ochre, are not only pleasing, but the combination supplies one of the GRAYS prevalent in nature.

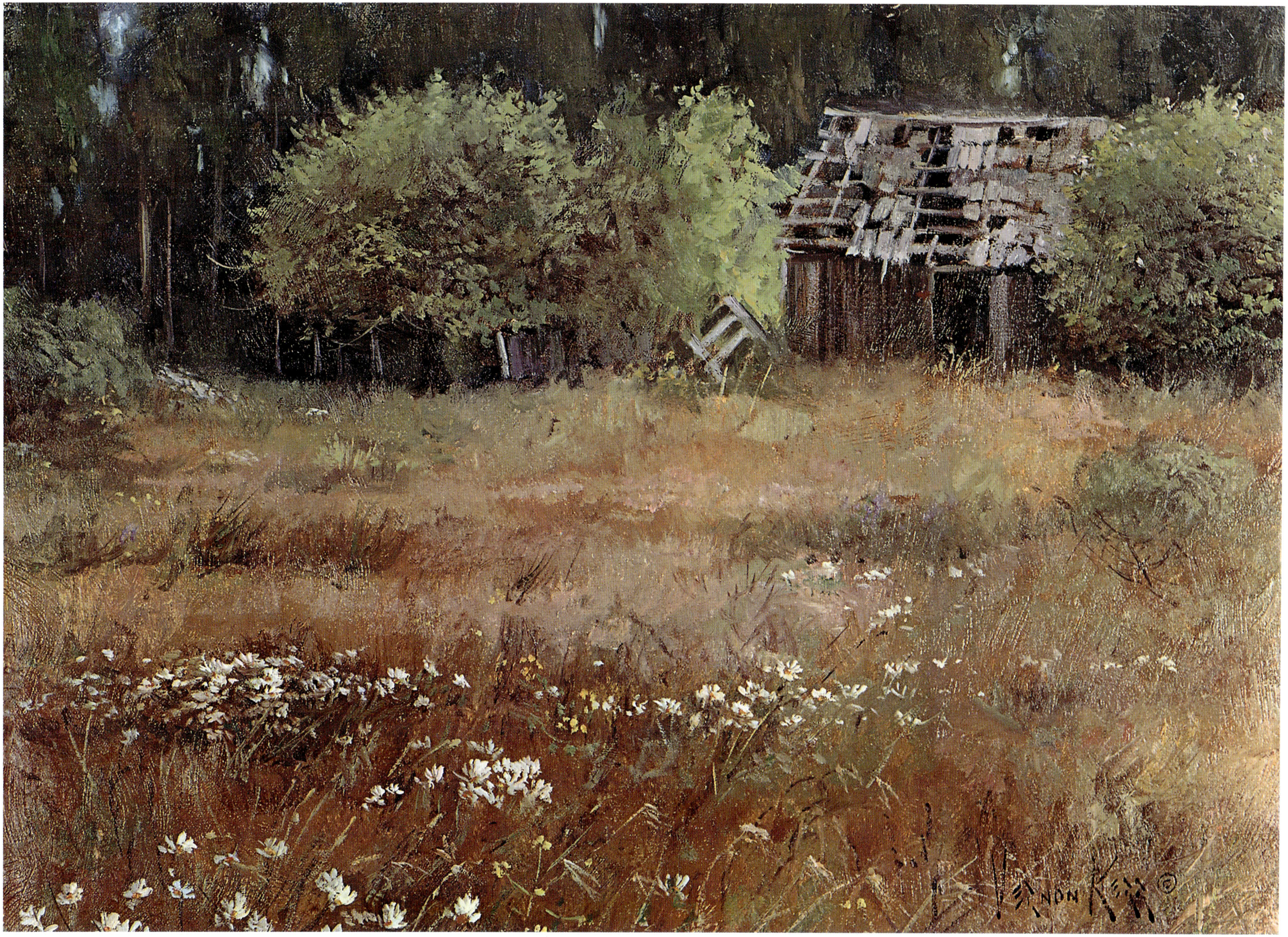

WALKING THROUGH SUMMER. I couldn't resist painting these old apple trees and barn. I pass it on the highway at least three times a week. Once in a while I see a deer feeding on the apples.

The interior darks of the barn are thin, rich, and warm in color. Do not paint the darks opaque. You want to be able to look into the shadows. Rembrandt was a master of this technique.

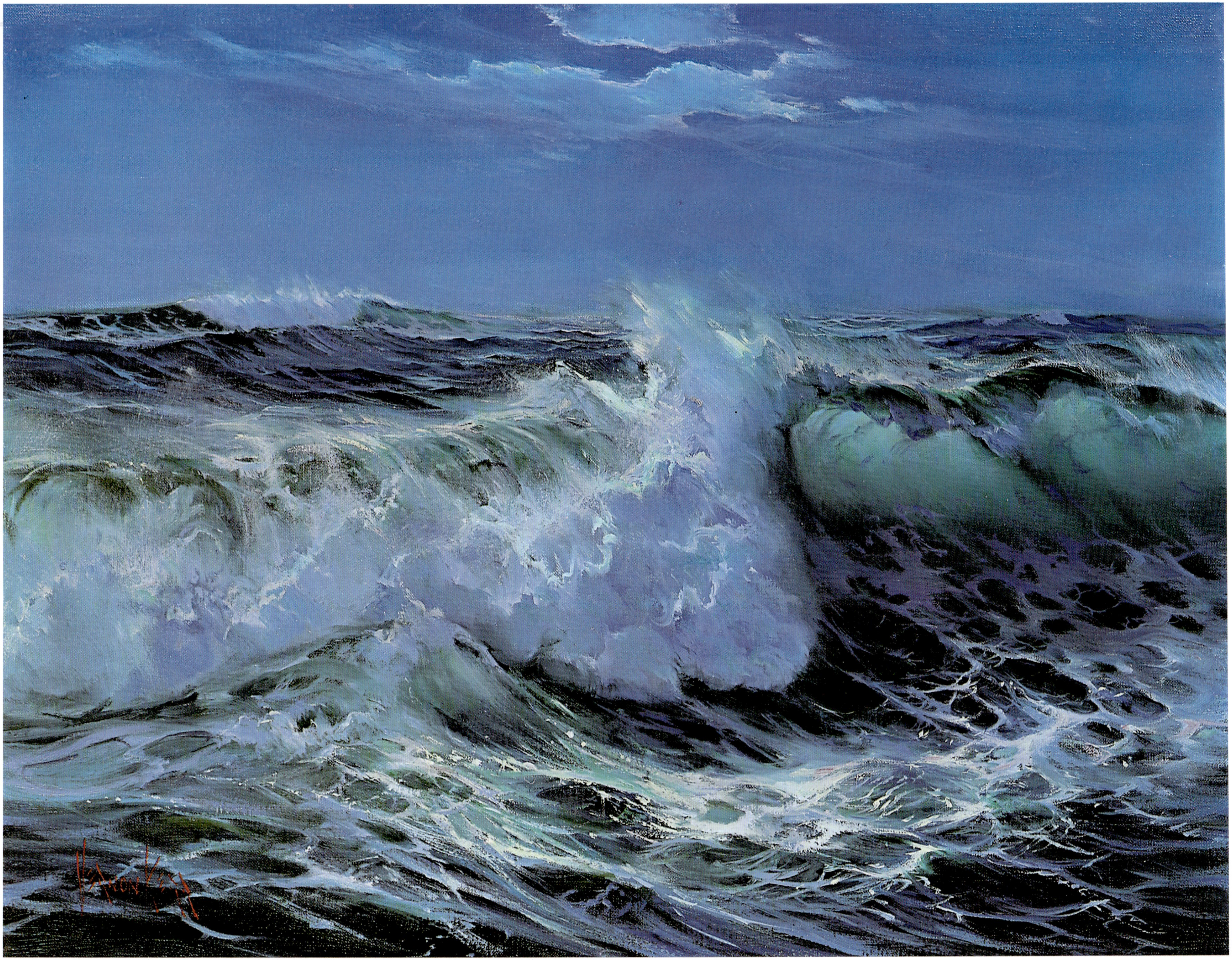

EVENING CHARM . . . *Vernon Kerr's paintings are featured in Haddads catalog of fine art reproductions.*

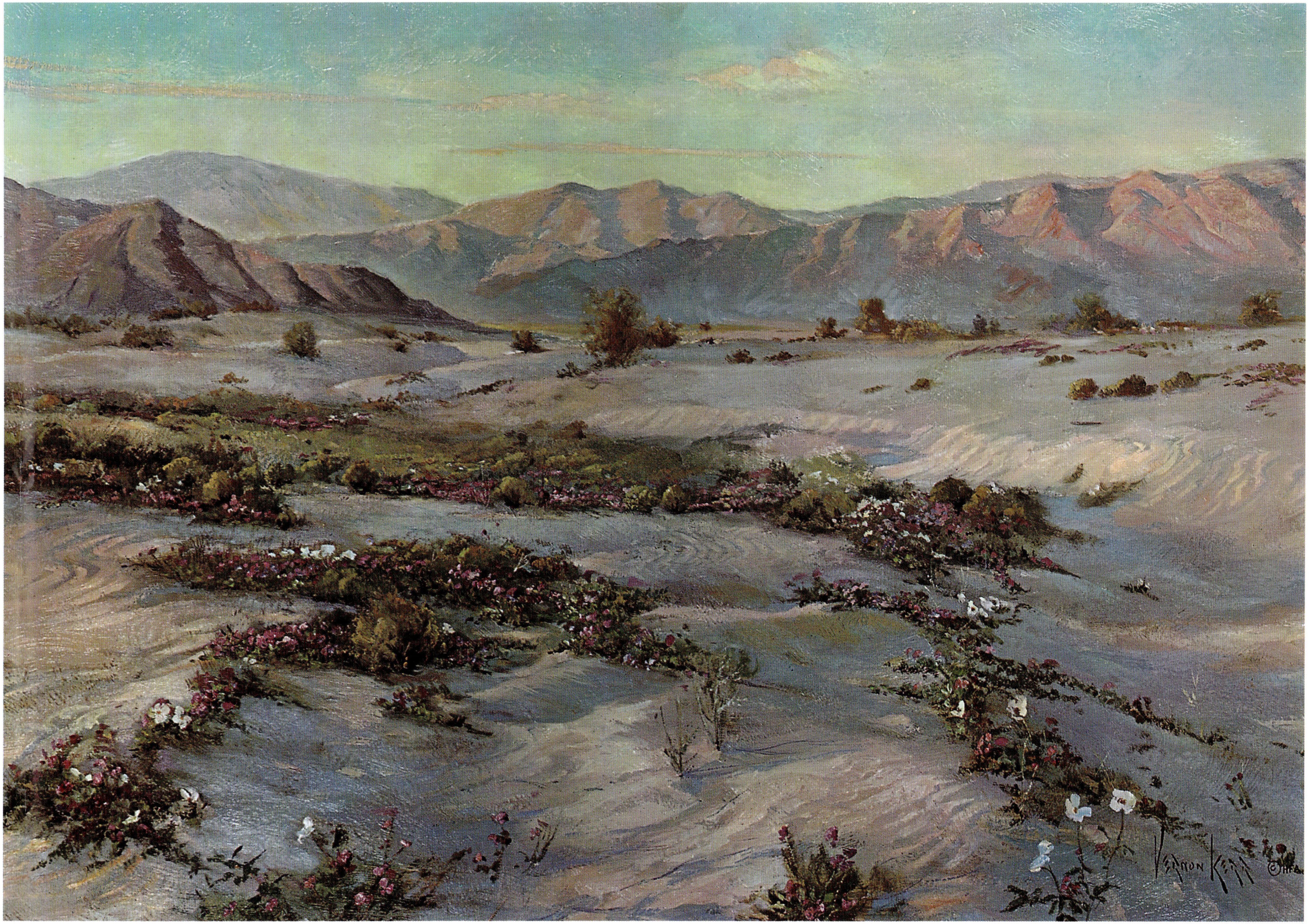

DESERT SPRING . . . *Courtesy of Haddads Fine Art Inc., Anaheim, Calif.*

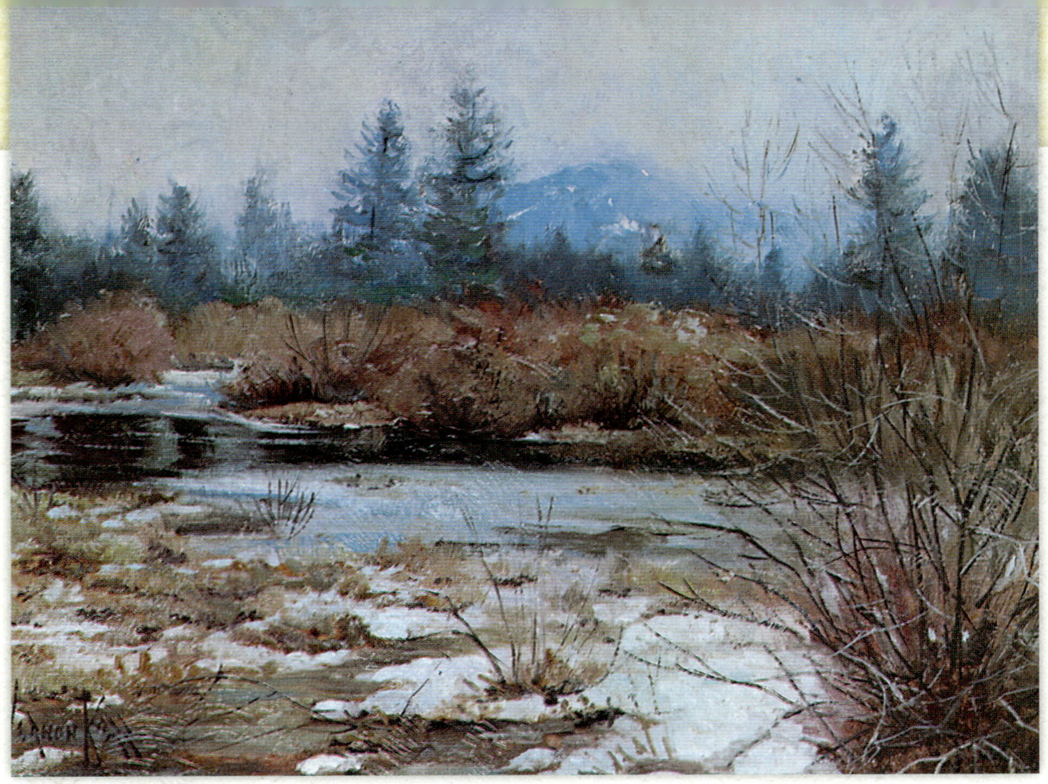

About the Artist

Vernon Kerr was born in Bellevue, Pennsylvania, in 1938. Recognizing his young son's talent, his father secured an apprenticeship for him with Leon Franks. Vernon studied with Franks for four years and was an accomplished artist by age 23. His first taste of fame occurred when he was the youngest artist to be published by the International Art Publishing Company. He worked as a naval illustrator while stationed in Japan during his time in the U.S. Navy and had also won numerous awards for his portraits, marines, and still lifes before his move to Laguna Beach, California, in 1959. In 1961 Vernon made headlines in the local newspaper after selling enough art during the town's annual art festival, that he was able to buy a truck and finance a trip across the country, painting along the way. Vernon was a professional artist for 26 years and was internationally known for his seascapes and landscapes. He taught at his own school in Laguna Beach and Coeur d'Alene, Idaho, for 15 years. He once said, "Painting is not fun unless I am learning something new, and nature is my greatest teacher." Vernon passed away in 1982 at the age of 44.